GLACIER GHOST STORIES

SPOOKY TALES AND LEGENDS FROM GLACIER NATIONAL PARK

KAREN STEVENS

RIVERBEND
PUBLISHING

Dedication
To my dear friend Mary Doerk of Fort Benton, Montana. May we have many more adventures together!

Glacier Ghost Stories
Copyright © 2013 by Karen Stevens
Published by Riverbend Publishing, Helena, Montana.

ISBN 978-1-60639-067-2

Many Glacier cover photo by Bruce Gourley, www.brucegourley.com
Lightning cover photo by Christopher Cauble, www.caublephotography.com
Ghost image by iStockphoto
Cover and text design by Sarah E. Grant, www.sarahegrant.com

RIVERBEND PUBLISHING
P.O. Box 5833
Helena, MT 59604
1-866-787-2363
www.riverbendpublishing.com

CONTENTS

PREFACE

Do you enjoy spooky stories about phantom figures and ghostly footsteps? Most people do. In fact, when the National Park Service surveyed Glacier National Park visitors to find out what they'd like added to park activities, many of them suggested ghost stories told around an evening campfire.

I've always been fascinated by ghosts. When I was seven years old my family moved into an old brick house in Minneapolis. It wasn't long before we realized that we were sharing the house with an invisible "something" that stomped up the basement stairs at night, turned lights on or off and rang doorbells. During the nineteen years we lived there, everyone in the family had experiences we couldn't logically explain. Eventually we learned to co-exist, though somewhat uneasily, with the ghost. Perhaps my early experiences led me to a career as a librarian, historian, and paranormal investigator.

For more than thirty years I've collected ghost stories from all over Montana. Many have appeared in *Haunted Montana: A Ghost Hunter's Guide to Haunted Places You Can Visit—If You Dare!* (2007) and its sequel, *More Haunted Montana* (2010), both published by Riverbend Publishing.

Among the stories I held back were several reports of eerie encounters in Glacier National Park. Even then it was clear that this most magnificent of parks, with its ghost stories and Native American legends, deserved a book of its own. I've visited Glacier and its neighbor to the north, Canada's beautiful Waterton Lakes National Park, many times over the past forty years—to hike, photograph wildlife and, of course, to search for even more stories of the uncanny and mysterious.

Are the great lodges of Glacier and Waterton really haunted? Who is the ghostly mountain man who walks down Going-to-the-Sun Road? Is there an explanation for the eerie drumbeats that sometimes echo through the forest at Trail of the Cedars? Why is Chief Mountain sacred to the Blackfeet? Do the shrieking winds of Marias Pass carry the cries of warriors slain in battle hundreds of years ago? Who—or what—is the forbidding presence at a remote backcountry campground?

Among the hundreds of people who have graciously shared their stories with me are the dedicated men and women of Parks Canada and the National Park Service, particularly seasonal ranger Doug Follett; employees of the great lodges, hikers, campers, wranglers, red-bus drivers, and tourists. Many thanks are owed to them, as well as authors Chris Morrison and Ray Djuff, true authorities on the parks, for their helpful suggestions.

To noted artist, historian, and member of the Blackfeet tribe Darrell Norman, *Ee-Nees-Too-Wah-See*, who helped me better understand the Blackfeet view of the spirit world, *Nehd-seh-nee-yeh'dahgi!* Thank you!

A warm note of appreciation is also due to the management of Glacier Park Inc. for their encouragement.

To legendary journalist and red-bus driver Robert Lucke, who incorporated ghost stories into his repertoire to the everlasting delight of tourists—many thanks!

To my longtime friend Pat Cody, who shares my love of adventure, a warm hug!

And a special tribute to the late Shellie Larios, whose *Yellowstone Ghost Stories* (Riverbend Publishing, 2006), inspired me to write this companion volume.

Enjoy!

INTRODUCTION

My love affair with Glacier National Park began more than forty years ago, when my husband and I checked into Many Glacier Hotel for the first of many visits. No matter how often I return, that first glimpse of Glacier's spectacular peaks reflected in Swiftcurrent Lake never fails to awe and delight. As naturalist John Muir wrote about Glacier, at that time still the Flathead Forest National Reserve, "*Give a month at least to this precious reserve. The time will not be taken from the sum of your life. Instead of shortening it, it will indefinitely lengthen it and make you truly immortal. Nevermore will time seem short or long, and cares will never again fall heavily on you, but gently and kindly as gifts from heaven.*"

Glacier National Park includes over 1500 square miles of pristine wilderness, 700 miles of trails, towering peaks, deep valleys, alpine lakes, waterfalls, rare alpine plants, hundreds of species of birds and animals including mountain goats and grizzly bears, and, of course, glaciers, although many have melted away in the last few decades. This remote and rugged wilderness was called the "Crown of the Continent" by the influential park advocate George Bird Grinnell and the "Backbone of the World" by the Blackfeet Indians. For at least eight thousand years, humans have left material traces of their passage through this rugged area, from crude stone shelters and tipi rings to abandoned nineteenth-century mines.

In 1910, an Act of Congress established Glacier as the nation's tenth national park, to protect its pristine environment, and in 1932, Glacier and Canada's neighboring Waterton Lakes National Park joined to become Waterton-Glacier International Peace Park. Waterton-Glacier is also a UNESCO World Heritage Site.

Glacier National Park is truly a national treasure. Like all our national parks, it offers people breathing space in a crowded world, while it protects fragile ecosystems. Perhaps biologist Sigurd F. Olson put it best: "Wilderness to the people of America is a spiritual necessity...a means of regaining serenity and equilibrium." Since Yellowstone was established as our first national park in 1872, over 287,000,000 people have visited the 58 parks in the national parks system.

Early travel brochures described Glacier National Park as magnificent, grand, spectacular, awesome, remote, spiritual, and even otherworldly. Playwright Mary Roberts Rinehart, who visited the park in 1915, wrote in *Through Glacier Park*, "*There is no voice in all the world so insistent to me as the wordless call of these mountains. I shall go back. Those who go once always hope to go back. The lure of the great free spaces is in their blood.*"

Roughly two million people visit Glacier National Park annually. Many of them return year after year to hike, fish, photograph wildlife, learn about native cultures, or simply relax. Perhaps those who loved the park strongly in life left something of themselves behind, for the park abounds with tales of ghostly encounters along ancient trails worn down by moccasined feet. Not long ago, for instance, a phantom in grimy buckskins was seen at twilight striding past the visitor center at St. Mary. Near Lake McDonald, drumbeats from the distant past are said to echo at times through a sacred grove of cedars. At Marias and Cut Bank passes, bloody battles between Native Americans in the late 1700s left unpleasant psychic residues that can sometimes be sensed by members of those tribes.

The great lodges have their tales too, of figures in old-fashioned clothing that are sometimes glimpsed in the corridors and in rooms they once knew well. At Belton Chalet, a man wearing a derby hat has been seen at the railroad station and in the lodge itself. Winter caretakers at Many Glacier Hotel report odd occurrences in the deserted building and during the summer season, someone—or something—calls the front desk from an unoccupied room to request towels. Lake McDonald Lodge once boasted a ghost that obligingly appeared on a third-floor balcony each afternoon—until it tripped over its sheet! Guests at one of the lodge's rustic cabins, however, reported hearing someone shuffle around the room during the night. No one was visible. At St. Mary Lodge and Resort, employees often find merchandise scattered across the floor of the gift shop in the morning. Housekeeping staff at Glacier Park Lodge have heard voices coming from an empty room in the Annex, and at Apgar Village Inn, housekeepers have watched drawers open and close by themselves in a particular room. And we can't forget Canada's Waterton Lakes National Park, adjoining Glacier to the north, with its world-famous Prince of Wales Hotel. Night auditors there have heard disembodied footsteps late at night on the second-floor balconies.

Even backcountry campgrounds can provide unexpected chills. Each summer for eleven years, Eric G. drove out from Wisconsin to backpack and do various types of work for and in the park. Although he spent many nights off trail in remote areas, only once did he experience anything unexpected:

> My companion and I arrived at Reynolds Creek campground late in the afternoon in early summer, good daylight yet, and were in good spirits looking forward to the trek. As we walked into the campground and checked out the tent sites (no one else was at the campground that night), we walked down a path to what turned out to be the most attractive site. The second we entered the site, my hair stood on end and I felt like we were being watched. The forest got suddenly quiet. The immediate feeling was that we did not belong there. I suggested we check out the other sites and slowly backed out. The feeling left and did not return in any of the other sites.

After selecting another site, my companion said she was re-lieved we did not pick the best one. When I asked why, she told me she had the same feeling I had and also felt we did not belong there. I should also add that I have had several run-ins with bears with a similar experience of feeling I was watched or hair on end but I always could smell the bear that was that close and I never had the feeling that I did not belong there. This experience was significantly different. There was definitely something there and I doubt I would go back to reaffirm.

Those who have felt the touch of the uncanny believe.

Will you?

APGAR VILLAGE INN

A COLD WIND CARRIED THE SCENT OF SNOW FROM THE HIGH peaks as we got out of our car at Apgar Village. It was early September, and Glacier National Park's brief summer was nearly over. Soon the visitors who crowded Apgar's motels, the gift shops and cafes would be gone, the campground empty, the summer cabins boarded up until the following spring. The tiny village just inside the west entrance to Glacier Park would sink into its winter dormancy, disturbed only by the occasional deer or visitor on snowshoes.

Apgar Village was named for Civil War veteran Milo Apgar, who settled at the foot of Lake McDonald in the early 1890s. The short growing season made farming unprofitable, so when the Great Northern Railroad built a depot and chalet at nearby Belton in 1910, Apgar and others began to offer lodging and boat tours of deep, glacially-carved Lake McDonald to tourists who wanted to see the just-established park. Apgar's original cabin still stands in the village named for him.

My friend Pat and I had driven down from Lake McDonald Lodge to inquire about a ghost story at the Apgar Village Inn. According to Phil, who maintains both properties for Glacier Park Inc., there had been some unusual occurrences in the manager's apartment and in two guest rooms at the Village Inn.

"The story is that about thirty or forty years ago, an older gentleman died in the tub in Room 66," Phil told us. "Since then, there are supposed to have been other unexplained incidents in the bathtub. One involved a suicide, and the other involved a young kid who died of a heart attack in that tub. This past winter we took out all the linoleum, and underneath the plywood there were still bloodstains. We believe it's where the boy with the heart attack died. He was apparently trying to get out of the tub and cut his arm on the towel bar while flailing around and that's where the blood came from."

Deaths do occur in hotels and motels, of course, but so far no historical evidence has been discovered to confirm any of the rumored deaths in Room 66. Whether or not the deaths actually occurred, however, Phil has certainly had some strange experiences in those rooms.

"As far as maintenance is concerned," he said, "ooms 66 and 67 are mirror images of each other, with bathrooms backing up to each other. If I get a call from the Village Inn, it's about one of those two rooms. They call me when there's a problem with a door lock. I go down there and it works just fine, I walk away and it doesn't work at all. Just as fast as I can go grab my tools and come back, it works fine again. I've replaced the door and the lock, everything! I'm thinking that it was a tweak in the lock, but it still happens. It's random, but always 66 and 67."

The Apgar Village Inn certainly doesn't resemble the Hollywood version of a "haunted house." Constructed in 1956, the well-kept two-story building sits just yards from the shore of beautiful Lake McDonald. The Inn was sold to the National Park Service in 1959 and added to the National Register of Historic Places in 1987. It is now operated by Glacier Park Inc. Although the motel's design is classic midcentury-modern, the deep brown color and decorative trim are evocative of the older lodges in the park.

As we approached the inn, one of Glacier's famous red tour buses arrived to pick up people waiting inside the office. We waited until the bus had departed before introducing ourselves to the inn's manager. He readily confirmed the stories of a possible haunting.

"I've worked here for four years," he told us. "A few times I've been woken up by light sounds and felt there was a presence in my bedroom. It was a very powerful feeling. The previous manager said he'd seen a lady walking up the stairs by candlelight at night, but I've never seen anything like that. For me it's about 4 A.M. Sometimes what sounds like a bell rings 'ding!' to wake me up."

But it was rooms 66 and 67 we really needed to check out, he said, echoing what Phil had told us. Housekeeping staff and even a few guests had reported strange occurrences in those rooms. If we walked over to the rooms, we might be able to talk to the housekeepers before they finished their work for the day.

Our timing couldn't have been better. The doors of both rooms stood open, and a laundry cart sat beneath the overhanging roof. The hum of a vacuum came from one of the rooms. We stepped cautiously inside the other, unoccupied room.

Room 67 resembled the cozy tourist cabins which were so popular in the 1950s and which can still be found in small towns even today. Although the inn's rooms are part of a long rectangular building rather than separate cabins, the layout was similar to the cabins I recalled from my childhood: wood-paneled walls, a pleasant kitchen and eating area, and a large sitting room/bedroom with two queen-size beds. Picture windows overlooked Lake Mc-Donald just a few yards away. Rustic deck chairs lined the porch outside, where guests can relax and enjoy the spectacular view on fine summer evenings. I could definitely picture myself sitting there with a refreshing glass of iced tea after a day's fishing or a gentle stroll along the beautiful Trail of the Cedars.

The noise of the vacuum in the room next door stopped suddenly, and a moment later two of the housekeeping staff came in. We introduced ourselves and explained that we had heard that the inn might be haunted. One of the women has worked for the Village Inn for eighteen years, the other for nine. Although they preferred to remain anonymous, they quickly confirmed that each had experienced some odd things in rooms 66 and 67.

"There's a foul odor in the bathroom sometimes," the long-time housekeeper said. "It smells like there's something dead in there. It's coming from the ceiling because when the fan's on, it gets worse and worse. Maintenance has climbed up and looked in, but nothing's ever there, no dead animals or anything. They've even taken out the vents to check. Sometimes it's just a faint odor, but the longer the fan is on, the worse it gets."

"How long has that been going on?" I asked curiously.

"Almost three years," she replied. "Some of the customers would go up to the office and complain about it."

She invited us to step into the bathroom, and turned on the fan for us. Unfortunately, she and her coworker had already cleaned the bathroom and at first, all I could smell was the cleaning solution they had used. After a few minutes, however, we noticed a faint, unfamiliar odor that seemed to be coming through the fan.

Mysterious odors are often reported in places reputed to be haunted. Sometimes the odors are pleasant, like the fragrance of baking bread or perfume, while other times they may be foul. Strangely enough, not everyone can smell them. To those who can, however, the odors are very real.

"If an animal got into the wall and died," I commented, "the smell wouldn't last more than a week or two. Definitely not for three years. And it wouldn't just come and go."

The housekeeper nodded. "I've had guests complain about noises in the wall, but it's always in 66, not 67. It could be critters, I suppose, but there's never anything in there. We can't figure it out."

We followed her over to Room 66. As Phil had mentioned, it was the mirror image of Room 67, with the two bathrooms backed up to each other. The bathroom in Room 66 had just been cleaned and looked perfectly normal to me, yet if legend could be believed, three guests had died here, one reputedly a suicide. I glanced at Pat, who is highly sensitive to atmosphere. She shook her head slightly to indicate that she sensed nothing unusual.

The housekeeper gestured at the bathroom floor. "When they pulled up the old linoleum last year," she said, "they found what looked like blood all over the wood, and it looked pretty fresh. Phil showed us pictures of it. I don't know if anyone ever died here though, and I've worked here eighteen years."

Staff and even guests have had some odd experiences in Room 66, according to both housekeepers. "We have problems with the lock a lot," she told us. "Guests are always getting their keys redone. Or they'll complain about noises, like someone moving around the room. And sometimes drawers will just open by themselves. I'll come out of the bathroom and they're open, or I'll be making a bed and the drawer will open. I'll say, 'Okay, that was weird,' and I'll go take a break."

"Do you just find them open, or have you actually seen them open?" I asked curiously.

"Both," she replied.

As we were about to leave, the housekeeper recalled another incident, this one involving the room numbers on the door.

"One time a girl slammed the door and a screw fell out of the sign. It slipped upside down so the room number read 99 instead of 66. We called Phil to come fix it, but he couldn't come right away. When we got here the next morning, the sign had turned back to 66 again by itself."

With a twinkle in her eye, the housekeeper admitted, "We kind of messed with it for a couple of days so he had to come back again to fix it."

Pat and I thanked the two housekeepers for sharing their stories and headed purposefully for the office to find out whether the two rooms were available that night. Ghostly activity is actually pretty rare, but even if nothing happened, what an adventure it would be to spend a night in those rooms!

As it turned out, Room 66 had already been reserved, but Room 67 was still available. We promptly booked it and let the manager know that if the reservation for Room 66 fell through, we'd take that one too.

We spent a leisurely hour that afternoon strolling along the Trail of the Cedars, a level boardwalk that winds through an ancient forest of towering cedar and hemlock trees just a few minutes' drive from Lake McDonald Lodge. The cathedral-like hush was broken only by the trickle of water over moss-covered rocks, and we instinctively kept our voices low. In the past, the Kootenai and other Native American tribes visited the area to dig roots that were woven into baskets. Fallen trees provided sheets of bark that were used for rudimentary shelters, and wood that could be easily carved into bowls. Echoes from those long-ago days may still resonate at times in the shadowy forest, for a hiker told us that he'd heard deep, slow drumbeats early one morning when no one else was on the trail. They continued for quite a while at an even tempo and seemed to come from "everywhere and nowhere." Curious, he tried to find their source, but gave up after searching the forest for about an hour.

Some have suggested the sounds were caused by grouse drumming, although they lacked the birds' characteristic flourish at the end. Seasonal Ranger Doug Follett speculated that the sounds may have drifted downwind from Avalanche Lake, set in a high glacier-carved bowl two miles away, where members of local Indian tribes sometimes go to practice their music. Blackfeet artist and historian Darrell Norman offered a third opinion.

"At night, near my home," Norman said, "when the wind is blowing in the right way, I have heard singing and drumming, but nothing is out there. It's just energies from the past."

Pleasantly tired after our hike, we returned to Room 67 toward evening, stopping just long enough to drop off our cameras. The room seemed unusually cold, and I thought I caught a faintly unpleasant odor in the living room. We opened a window to let the room warm up, and headed over to Eddie's Café for supper.

The café is famous for its pies so, on the way, we discussed what we'd like to have for dessert. I told Pat that I wanted to try a local specialty, huckleberry pie. The pie was delicious, as were the Reuben sandwiches on marbled rye. Comfortably full, we returned to our kitchenette. The odor I'd noticed just before we'd left for supper was gone and the room temperature felt normal.

We made ourselves a pot of tea and settled contentedly in the Adirondack chairs facing Lake McDonald. Small boats bobbed gently at anchor and a few teenagers were splashing in the shallows of the placid lake. It was an idyllic evening. As the sun dropped behind the mountains, the afterglow tinted high cirrus clouds a delicate pink before slowly fading. Stars began to appear, and later the full moon rose over the mountains. We were reluctant to leave the peaceful scene but finally headed indoors to see if we could capture ghostly voices (Electronic Voice Phenomena, or EVP) on our digital recorder.

As far back as the 1920s, paranormal researchers attempted to record voices of the dead—with some apparent success. Modern researchers generally use hand-held tape recorders or digital recorders. I usually carry my digital recorder in an outside pocket of my purse. I hadn't realized, however, that the recorder had been running while Pat and I walked over to Eddie's Café for supper. When I played it back, we got quite a surprise.

Moments after I had told Pat that I wanted huckleberry pie for dessert, an elderly male voice had replied emphatically, "No way!" There had been only a few people on the street at the time and no one closer than thirty yards or so, yet the voice sounded as though whoever had spoken had been right beside us.

Had one of the spirits of the Village Inn followed us over to the café?

We sat down at our kitchen table and began to ask questions, hoping that the ghost—if there was one—would reply. Half an hour passed with no answer. Meanwhile, a sudden wind storm came up and the flower baskets outside our door began to sway. We went outside to watch, leaving the recorder running. A small boat had broken loose from its mooring and beached itself while another had disappeared, possibly sunk. Pat grabbed her camera and tried a few time exposures before we went back in to resume our interrupted EVP session. First, though, I replayed the few minutes that had been recorded while we were outside. To our surprise, we heard someone chuckle. It sounded like the same older male voice, slightly husky, that had said "No way!" when I announced that I planned to have huckleberry pie for dessert.

Nothing further happened that night, and we slept well, lulled by the noise of waves crashing onto the pebbly shore. By morning the wind had dropped and the lake was merely choppy, but dark gray clouds hung ominously above the peaks. We had planned to head over Going-to-the-Sun Road that morning, and we knew that the weather at six thousand feet could change from minute to minute. We packed up quickly. As we got into my car, on impulse I turned to wave farewell to the spirit of the man whose voice was on our recorder. I like to think of him as he may have been in life, relaxing in one of the Adirondack chairs after a day's fishing, perhaps recalling with pleasure the dessert he'd had that evening.

I'm pretty sure it wouldn't have been huckleberry pie.

BELTON CHALET

WE ARRIVED AT BELTON CHALET LATE ONE AFTERNOON AS A chilly drizzle began to fall. Mist clung to the slopes of the nearby mountains, and the scent of fresh snow on the highest peaks was unmistakable although it was only mid-August. It looked like a perfect night to curl up in chairs around a blazing fire and tell ghost stories. And there are plenty of stories to be told about the ghosts of Belton Chalet. Newspaper and magazine accounts of the haunting are prominently displayed on the walls of the game room in the basement and along the second floor corridor. Would we experience anything spooky during our overnight stay? We certainly hoped so!

There are no elevators in this century-old lodge, so my husband Frank, friend Sue, and I carried our luggage up the stairs. My husband and I had been given Room 31, and Sue had Room 35, just down the hall. The rooms turned out to be spacious, if rustic, with comfortable beds and private baths. There were no telephones or televisions to distract from the beautiful scenery outside the windows. I stood for a moment staring at the dripping forest behind the lodge and wondered how many other guests over the long years had stood in front of that window, gazing at the same scenery. For a moment the past seemed very close.

Belton Chalet is the oldest of several grand hotels built by the Great Northern Railway at Glacier and Waterton Lakes national parks. The complex of Swiss-style buildings was constructed between 1910 and 1913 to provide accommodations for tourists who arrived by rail. Guests could explore Glacier by stagecoach, aboard lake steamers, or on horseback, and return at night to the comfort of a blazing fire and excellent cuisine.

During construction of Going-to-the-Sun Road in the 1930s, Belton Chalet served as a dorm for work crews from the Civilian Conservation Corps. The lodge closed at the beginning of World War II when travel declined and the chalet was eventually sold. It went through several changes of ownership before Andy Baxter and Cas Still bought the old buildings in 1993 and restored them to their former grandeur. They are now a National Historic Landmark.

During the renovation, a number of strange things happened. Furniture would move around by itself, and muffled noises were heard coming from empty rooms. On one occasion, smudges that resembled the black soot left by kerosene lanterns were found covering walls that had just been painted. Perhaps some of Belton's former guests had returned to the lodge they had enjoyed so much in life.

Chalet staff searched through old records, but found no tragic events that might have accounted for a haunting. There are legends, of course: that a man was killed by a train across from the chalet; that a woman despondent over a love affair threw herself from a ledge behind the buildings, or that the chalet was built on an Indian burial ground. So far no historical basis for the haunting has been found.

Christie Roberts, general manager of the lodge, had agreed to meet us at the restaurant after dinner and share some of her experiences. We had plenty of time to explore the lodge from the creaking top-floor corridor to the huge stone fireplace to the game room with the colorful arts-and-crafts windows in the basement. By then the drizzle had settled into a light rain, and hikers were beginning to straggle in, wet and muddy. Just before five, we went back upstairs to our rooms to grab our jackets. Barely a minute later Sue knocked urgently at our door.

"The hot water was running in my sink!" she said. "I'm sure it was off when I left."

I followed her to her room and touched the taps. Sue had turned off the faucet, but it still felt very hot, indicating that it had been running for a long time. Fortunately, the sink had not overflowed. Sue's belongings had not been disturbed and there was no sign that anyone had been in her room.

We decided to report what appeared to be a problem with the plumbing, only to hear the lady ahead of us at the front desk report that the same thing had happened in her room just down the hall from Sue's room.

"There was no damage," the other guest assured the desk clerk. "It didn't overflow."

The clerk nodded. "We've been getting a lot of that this year," she answered matter-of-factly. She told us that the plumbing had been updated during renovations just a few years before, but lately a number of guests had found water running in their sinks. Others reported that the valve beneath the sink had been shut off. The rooms had been locked and unoccupied at the time. It had happened too often to be mere forgetfulness on the part of guests.

"We think it's a mischievous ghost," the clerk said. I asked hopefully whether anything odd had occurred in our rooms, but the clerk shook her head. Most of the activity seemed to be concentrated in rooms 30 and 37.

"A female guest in Room 30 reported a woman weeping in her room all night," she said. "She told management the next day that she couldn't see anything but she could feel her and hear the weeping. She didn't know how to comfort her, so she started praying for her. A night auditor also heard the weeping late one winter night. It seemed to come from Room 37 that time. He was the only one in the building." Then she added helpfully, "One guest did say that he was touched on the shoulder as he sat up in bed."

I couldn't help but shiver at the thought. All of a sudden, snuggling up in a warm bed didn't seem as appealing as usual!

It was nearly time to meet Christie Roberts, so we hurried through the rain to the nearby restaurant, built in 1910 as the original Belton Chalet and now called the Tap. Roberts arrived with financial manager Mary Pete just as we finished an excellent dinner. The two women spend the winter by themselves at Belton Chalet and are well aware of the ghostly activity.

"There may be as many as six ghosts," Roberts told me. "There's a man wearing a derby hat who's been seen in Room 37 and at the train station. Guests have heard doors slamming and ghostly voices calling their names."

Mary Pete's husband was one of the workmen who encountered something odd during renovation in 1998. He had brought their dog to keep him company one day, and he noticed the dog was sitting at the foot of the stairs staring intently at the landing. No one was visible, but suddenly a child's marble came bouncing down the stairs. "My husband picked it up," Pete said. "It was an old Chinese marble. We still have it at the lodge."

"Once I was moving furniture on the second floor of the chalet and was locked into the bathroom," Pete said. "I couldn't open the door. Another employee had to let me out.

"I can smell the ghost," she added. "It's a sort of geriatric smell. Sometimes he follows me around."

Roberts agreed. "Mary smelled him up on the second floor one night, and she said he'd followed her down. I could smell him too."

"One night," Pete continued, "the employees at the Tap were sitting around the fireplace after closing and they heard the door of the walk-in cooler open and shut in the basement. They went down to check and no one was there."

Employees who stay in the rooms above the restaurant have also encountered Belton's ghosts. "We were doing a special event a couple of winters ago and I was working late," Roberts told me. "I had to be up early the next morning so I decided to sleep in the chalet above the restaurant. I knew I would only get four or five hours sleep and there were no alarm clocks in the room, so I asked the night auditor to knock on my door and wake me at seven A.M. I was exhausted so I went right to bed, but I kept hearing footsteps coming to my door. I thought it was Carmen coming to wake me up, so I'd wait for the knock. No knock came, and I'd go back to sleep, only to wake up again when footsteps came to the door. It happened three or four times during the night. I was the only one in the building that night, so I thought it had to be Carmen doing her night walk through the property.

"The next morning I heard the knock and got up and said to Carmen, 'Were you walking around up there last night? I heard you come to my door several times.'

"She said, 'No, I didn't even go down there once.'

"About six months later, I had a bartender who stayed up in the chalet. In the middle of the summer, she came down to the bar and said, 'I am freaked out!' She was up all night because someone kept walking up to her door. She could hear heavy boots. There was no knock, and nothing happened. She looked under the door and couldn't see shoes or a shadow. It freaked her out so bad that she ran out of the other door and out of the building. The Civilian Conservation Corps workers used to stay here in the old days, so maybe it was someone who used to wake them up."

On occasion, guests in the lodge have also had visits from Belton's spirits. According to Robert Lucke, a veteran red-bus driver who has collected many of the park's ghostly tales, the man in the derby hat is said to resemble Louis Hill, son of James J. Hill, founder of the Great Northern Railway. Another ghost is said to be a little Indian girl in buckskins who knocks on doors at night.

If followed, she leads guests to the stairway, where she vanishes.

In 2010, a female guest in Room 23 was awakened by heavy footsteps going from the balcony door towards the room door. She opened her eyes and the footsteps stopped. Her husband was still asleep and no one else was in the room. She closed her eyes again. The footsteps resumed. It happened three or four times before the footsteps faded away and didn't return.

Another couple also had an unexpected encounter with restless spirits. They couldn't sleep because they could hear people walking around in the room above them. They asked the night auditor, who sits at the front desk all night, to request the people in the room above them to quiet down. She told them that they were the only guests at the lodge that night and unlocked the room above theirs so they could see for themselves that the room was empty. They packed their bags and left.

Guests in Room 20 also came downstairs late one night to ask for help from the night auditor. According to them, someone had been jumping up and down on the bed in the next room and the noise was keeping them awake. The night auditor accompanied them back upstairs and showed them that the room next to theirs was a closet, not a bedroom, although it may have been part of a bedroom before the building was remodeled.

A guest who stayed at the lodge in July 2008 sent a letter to Belton describing the night that she had awakened to find a visitor sitting in a chair in her room. He was surrounded by a light that made it easy for her to make out his features. She described him as handsome, with dark hair and a muscular build. He told her that he was a miner and that he couldn't leave Glacier. She thought he said his name was Lundgren or something similar. He had heard her on the phone outside, and just wanted to assure her that she would survive whatever personal problems she was facing at the time. Christy sent the guest's letter over to a local family with a similar name, but they did not recognize the miner's description.

Another guest who stayed on the second floor in 2003 wrote that he had gotten up to go to the bathroom about 1:30 A.M. When he came out, he saw a large black cloud in front of the bathroom door. It moved away as he approached. At about 5 A.M. he again went to the bathroom. Once more, the black cloud was waiting for him outside the door. The guest stated that the cloud was roughly shaped like a large person and seemed interested in observing him. The guest returned to bed and the cloud eventually disappeared into the back wall. When he and his wife went downstairs in the morning, they discovered the newspaper articles about Belton's ghosts. The guest concluded by stating that he'd never seen a ghost before but had felt no fear during the encounter, just amazement at what had occurred.

Not all guests react to an encounter with Belton's ghosts so matter-of-factly. Night auditor Noreen Hanson was on duty early one morning in August 2009. "A woman came into the lobby and said that when her husband was showering, he turned around and there was a small girl in white standing in the shower. He yelled and jumped out. Shortly after that they both came to the front desk with their suitcases, gave me the key, and left. His hair was still wet. I went into the room but didn't see anything."

Hanson has also encountered a mischievous ghost the staff calls "Bob."

"One morning at 5 A.M., I was sitting at the desk upstairs when I heard a radio turn on somewhere. I thought somebody had set it to wake them up. I waited for someone to turn it off, but they didn't, so I thought I'd better go investigate before it woke everybody up. It seemed to be coming from the basement. I went down and found that the radio in the corner had been turned on. I said, 'Bob, that's not nice, people are sleeping,' and the kitchen doors flew wide open by themselves.

"A couple of weeks ago I found a paper jam in the copy machine in the basement. A stack of paper had been run through.

I pulled out the copies, but there was nothing on them. Maybe "Bob" has an infatuation with the copying machine.

"Although I've never seen him, I've felt him. I was sitting in my chair one day, and all of a sudden I got cold chills up the back of my neck. All I could do was say, 'Good morning to you too, Bob!'"

Belton's employees agree that paranormal activity seems to pick up in the autumn, though perhaps it's just more noticeable without the hustle and bustle of summer guests. Certainly the chalet offers a rare opportunity for ghost hunters who would like to spend a night or two skulking along creaking corridors looking for ghosts.

Did one of Belton's "permanent residents" put in an appearance during our visit? Although I woke several times during the night and lay listening to the creaks of the old lodge, we were not disturbed.

There's always next time.

GLACIER PARK LODGE

JUST BEFORE TEN ON A BEAUTIFUL SEPTEMBER MORNING, OUR train eased to a halt at East Glacier Station. Pat and I had stayed the previous night at the Izaak Walton Inn, an historic railroad hotel at Essex on the southern edge of the park, and rode Amtrak's sleek silver Empire Builder that morning on the scenic ride back to East Glacier and the haunted Glacier Park Lodge. As we left the platform, the train's horn signaled imminent departure, and we turned to wave farewell to the remaining passengers.

We hadn't far to walk. Just across the road from the depot stands majestic Glacier Park Lodge, surrounded by beautifully landscaped grounds and beds of colorful flowers. The lodge opened on June 15, 1913, with ceremonies attended by hundreds of Blackfeet and other guests. They must have felt a sense of awe when they stepped for the first time into the immense five-story lobby supported by massive 500-year-old Douglas-fir tree trunks. *Omahkoyis*, or Big Tree Lodge, as the Blackfeet named it, still impresses modern visitors with its grandeur.

No wonder some of the lodge's long-departed guests are said to linger in some of the corridors and rooms!

Robert Lucke, the Red Bus driver who sought out many of the park's ghost stories, told us that much of the ghostly activity at Glacier Park Lodge occurs in the Great Northern Wing, known as the Annex. Built in 1914, the four-story wing quickly became a favorite with wealthy families, many of whom reserved their favorite suites year after year. In hopes of encountering some of the lodge's fabled spirits, Pat and I had booked Room 208 room in the Annex for the night.

According to Lucke, ghostly activity is more likely to be noticed when employees are getting the hotel ready to open in the spring or closing it up in the fall. Carrie, a restaurant server who has worked at Glacier Park Lodge for four seasons, agreed, and told me about an encounter with the lodge's invisible residents during her second season. At that time she worked in housekeeping and helped to open the lodge in the spring.

"It's scary and creepy in the empty building," she recalled. "When my best friend Liz and I opened this one room on the second floor of the Annex for the first time, all the furniture was pushed against the wall like it normally is. We opened some more rooms and then we walked back to the first room. All the furniture in that room had been pushed to the center of the room.

"I thought someone was playing a prank on us, but those floors are so creaky, and there was just us on the floor, we'd have heard something. We didn't hear anything. We ran down to our housekeeping manager and she said, 'Sometimes these things happen. We'll be smudging the room so you won't have to worry about anything.'" According to Native American tradition, negative energies may be cleansed from a place by smudging or censing with burning sage.Intrigued, Pat and I talked with Sanny, head of the housekeeping department, about her experiences. Sanny has worked at the lodge for many years and confirmed that opening the lodge for the season can be unsettling.

"I came on as a room attendant," she said in her soft voice. "One day we split up as teams and started opening the lodge. We started on the suites in the Annex. There were two of us. She was on the mountain side and I was on the garden side. As I was cleaning the shower floor, I felt like someone was right there. I looked but didn't see anyone. I just kept cleaning, but I could still feel a presence on the side of me. I wanted to clean as fast as I could and get out. Finally I said, 'I'm just here to do my job, and I'm not here to bother anyone.'

"My assistant manager came by and said it was break time so we stepped out on the veranda by Room 228 where she was cleaning. One side of the veranda door was still locked, and the other side was open. We checked the door so we wouldn't be locked out. I stayed right by the glass door because it was cold, it was springtime. I stood there while she smoked and when we turned around to go back in we were locked out. You have to dead bolt it and I was standing right there. I would have heard it click. We were shocked. We went to the other door, and that was still locked, so we were stuck out there. We tried the window of 228 but it was locked. We couldn't go down, only up on the fire escape ladder, but no one was on the third floor yet, so the doors were obviously locked. We started yelling at people in cars, but they didn't even look up.

"All we could do was bang on the door. Well, we were lucky that day that someone was bringing up supplies from the warehouse and he heard us banging. We said, 'Why did you lock us out? It's not funny. We have a lot of work to do!'

"He said, 'Hey, I just got here. I just brought the supplies.'

"I've heard stories about Room 316. When you go in, to the right there's a big closet. I always felt strange about that closet even before I heard the stories. One morning I went up there to check the rooms. I went over to 316 and knocked on the door and said, 'Housekeeping,' and a real light female voice said, 'I'm in here.' I looked at my printout that showed which rooms are occupied, and it wasn't occupied. I went to a house phone across the hall and called the front desk and asked if they had checked anyone in after the printout had been done. They said they hadn't. I knocked again at 316. No one answered. I went into the room and looked around and it was unoccupied.

"My adopted son was a bellman, and early one morning he took baggage from late check-ins up to the third floor. It was about 3 A.M., so he took it up the stairs. He got midway up the stairs and saw a lady standing at the top there. She looked really upset with him. He took two more steps and got to the top and she was gone. She was wearing a long, old-fashioned dress.

"Another time I was pushing my cart along and I saw this lady walking. She was coming down the hall very slowly. I saw her go into Room 307. She was an older lady with curled short white hair. I went into 310 and started cleaning it. When I came out two minutes later, I checked my clipboard and it said Room 307 was unoccupied, but I saw her open the door and go in. So I knocked and said, 'Housekeeping,' and it was unoccupied.

"One day I was in Room 305 inspecting it. I inspected the bathroom first, closed the bathroom door and looked around the room, and I'm done with this room. Just as I was going out, the bathroom door opened. I thought, *okay*, and didn't look back.

"In one of the suites, we had just done the room, but when we went back to check, the bed was undone. There were also two wet prints of pointed shoes in the bathroom. We could not explain that. Once they were painting on third in the hallways and we went up to check their work. All the furniture was out of 316 and in the hallway. I thought they were doing maintenance but we looked in the room and there was no maintenance. The chair was on the desk. Maybe somebody wanted the room painted.

"There's supposed to be a young girl in 316 who killed herself over a broken heart and a ghostly gentleman by the fireplace on the third floor. He likes to stay there. There are two spirits in 228, an older man and a younger one. The older one is overbearing. He stands by a window overlooking the pool. The younger one stays back by the bathroom. The older one doesn't want to let the young one go. And in the Moccasin Room on the basement level, there are two ghostly men by the old bar."

At least one of the spirits in the hotel is a prankster. According to another employee, a gentleman who stayed there several years ago always put his shoes under the bed. When he got up one morning, his shoes were gone. He looked all over for them and couldn't find them. Finally he looked back under the bed and his shoes were there, but they were two sizes too small!

Pat and I love to browse in gift shops wherever we travel. Not only does the shop at Glacier Park Lodge offer the usual guidebooks, tasty jams, and souvenirs, but an occasional brush with the uncanny as well. Franklin, a Navajo working his third season in the shop, told us about an experience he'd had several times during his second season.

"It always happened around closing, after all the customers had left," he said. "I'd shut down the gate and the door on the other side of the gift shop and turn off all the light switches, then head to the door. There was only one light on to guide me. I would come to this side from the other aisle, and that's when the chill would start. It felt like someone was right behind me but I knew nobody was there. I wouldn't even look around, just walked a little faster."

A clerk who had been quietly listening spoke up. "When I first came to Glacier Park Lodge, I was just overpowered," she said. "It was like the ghosts were playing tricks on us. This year I was walking past a display and all of a sudden I saw someone pass me by and the shirts started moving like someone had brushed past them. No one was there."

Sheli, the long-time manager of the gift shop, has had more than a few encounters with the ghost.

"When we leave at night, we sweep and vacuum," she told us. "Sometimes when we come in the next morning, there will be toys in the center of the room. It happens all year long. It's like a standing joke. One time, one of the toys came off the shelf, just straight out. A customer and another lady saw it. The customer looked at the other lady and said, 'Did you just see a stuffed animal go across the room?'

"The other lady said, 'Yes, I saw it.' 'Okay,' the customer said, 'then we're not crazy.'

"I've been here for nine years," Sheli continued, "and it's been going on that long. I've been through two cleansings by the Blackfeet, and things straighten out for a while."

She led us over to a wooden statue of an Indian that stood near the doorway. Tourists often pose for photos with the statue, and some of them have commented that the stern-faced statue seems to be smiling in the photos. Naturally, Pat and I tried our luck. Sure enough, the statue did seem to be smiling. Was it a trick of the light? Flash bounce? Try a photo or two and see what you think!

According to Sheli, the statue has been in the gift shop for a long time. "A gentleman came in last year and asked to speak to the manager," she said. "He told me that he had a confession to make. Forty years ago when he was five years old, his parents had given him a pocket knife, and when they brought him in here, he cut the Indian.

"He had his picture taken with it. Then he said, 'Are we even?' I assured him we were.

"The statue and I are good friends," she added. "When I leave here at the end of the year, I miss him."

Although ghostly activity happens around the clock, employees who work the night shifts have the best chance of encountering something eerie, perhaps because hotels are quiet during the dark hours. Kathie, the front desk manager, told us, "From about 3 a.m. to 4:30 or so it gets really eerie in here. One night I heard something I looked up, and saw a little girl standing on the third floor balcony looking at me. She had long black hair. She stood there for three, maybe four minutes just looking, and I got so uneasy that I went into my office. When I came out, she was gone."

"Security Renee," as she likes to be called, is the head of the hotel's security department. She's worked there for five seasons, and each season brings new adventures. We caught up with her that evening after she and a coworker captured a bat that had strayed into a guest room.

Renee hadn't heard many ghost stories about the lodge before she started working there, but she's not afraid of spirits. "As a Native American," she explained, "we rely on the spirits for protection."

Her first season at the lodge was spooky. Housekeeping employees were working on the third floor of the annex one day, and most of the room doors stood open. As Renee walked past one of the rooms, the door suddenly slammed.

"I thought there must be a window open," she said, "so I opened up the room with a universal key and there was no window open. If you step on a certain board in the annex, it will creak way down the hall, so I walked around the hall to see if I had stepped on a floorboard that made the door slam, but I couldn't find any. I left the door open and as soon as I went down the hall the door slammed again. That was Room 316.

"I told one of the guys in maintenance the story and he said back in the 1950s there was a young lady in housekeeping who was in love with one of the guys. He rejected her and she hung herself in that room. I don't know if there's any validity to it."

Like any old building, the lodge has its repertoire of natural noises. Renee is frequently called to assure new employees that wooden floors do creak as the building cools at night, heaters make popping sounds when they come on, and when the wind rises, the skylights high overhead will rattle. But every now and then, something happens that can't be explained so easily.

"That same season my partner and I were walking past the gift shop about 2:30 A.M.," Renee told us. "There's a statue of an Indian in the doorway, and the eyes looked like they were moving. My partner saw it too. Just as we got close enough to take a good look, the music box that plays Indian flute music started playing. All the lights were out in the shop. We unlocked the door and went in. The music box was unplugged, but it was still playing music. When we looked up, the music stopped. We both got creeped on that one.

"Another time during the first season we had a gentleman who came to the front desk about 3 A.M. He was in 316. He said, 'Are there ghosts here?'

"I happened to be there, and I said, 'Oh, there's nothing to be afraid of, sir.'

"He said, 'I was in bed and thought I heard footsteps in my room. I turned on my light, and when I did, the chair from my desk just came out. Then my door opened. I thought I saw someone walk out and the door closed, so I came down here to ask if it's haunted.'

"So I said, 'Well, we've had things happen, but we've never had anyone harmed.'

"Just this season, as I was delivering some ice at 2 A.M. to a guest who had just checked into 202, there was a huge shadow that looked like it had a cowboy hat on. It went through the wall of 224. I felt the hair on my neck just stand up as I went by that room.

"One time I was on the second floor of the annex when all of a sudden there was a lady in front of me. I'm always looking around because that's what I'm trained to do, but I hadn't seen her. I thought, 'Where did she come from?'

"She was in old-timey clothing, maybe 1930s or 1940s. I went all the way to the end of the floor and turned around and came back again, and there she was again, ahead of me. I thought, 'How come I don't hear footsteps? How come the floor isn't creaking for her like it's creaking for me?' She turned and went up the steps to the third floor. I went up the stairs behind her, doing every other step to stay right behind her, but I didn't see her feet. She looked like she was floating. As soon as she turned the corner, she was gone.

"One of the girls working down in the annex had just finished cleaning an empty room and was putting dirty laundry in a bag when she saw a little girl sitting there swinging her legs on the bed. It scared her, so she took off. She also saw the same lady I did and described her to a T."

Renee believes that many of the spirits that roam Glacier Park may be those of Native Americans. "This land was all Blackfeet territory, so there were many little wars going on and many Indians were killed. You're going to have spirits wandering not only in the lodges, but all over."

We thanked Renee for sharing her experiences and went to our room on the second floor of the Annex. For a while we sat on the porch, listening to sleepy chirps as birds settled down for the night. Would the spirits of those who roamed the park long ago haunt our dreams?

Apparently they had better things to do. We woke early after an undisturbed night.

Perhaps next time we'll ask for Room 316.

GOING-TO-THE-SUN ROAD

IT WAS MID-AFTERNOON WHEN PAT AND I LEFT THE VISITOR CENTER at Logan Pass. The dark gray clouds that had obscured the peaks at Apgar earlier had descended almost to road level. At an altitude of 6,646 feet, the weather can change in an instant—and often does. One year, I saw snow flurries at Logan Pass on the Fourth of July.

Although I've driven across Going-to-the-Sun Road many times since my first visit in 1971, the narrow two-lane Sun Road can be nerve-racking. When the visibility is minimal, even those who know the cliff-hugging road well may experience a few white-knuckle moments. Throw in the presence of heavy road equipment at construction zones, few guardrails, and a road scraped bare to rain-slicked rock, and it can get tense.

Over the years, torrential rains, heavy mountain snows, avalanches and rockslides had badly damaged stone retaining walls, drainage systems, and pavement. In 2007, after a decade of careful study and planning, a massive ten-year rehabilitation project got underway. Although Going-to-the-Sun Road remained open to traffic during the short summer seasons, drivers were advised to expect brief delays at construction zones.

Sure enough, a few miles east of Logan Pass we were flagged down to wait for a pilot car to guide us through the construction zone. Most drivers ahead of us got out of their cars to stretch their legs and enjoy the spectacular view of soaring mountains, cascading waterfalls and lush forests. The low stone guard-walls at the side of the road had been removed so their crumbling foundations could be repaired. Now the only thing between us and the dizzying fall to the valley floor below was an orange traffic cone. Going-to-the-Sun Road has seen many fatalities over the years, and I edged nervously away from that long, long drop. Some of the other drivers were making determined efforts not to look down either, and not all of them had flatlander license plates.

Automobiles were still rare when Glacier became a national park in 1910. Most visitors arrived by train at Midvale (now East Glacier) or Belton (now West Glacier). The only road inside the new park was a barely-passable wagon trail connecting Belton to the village of Apgar. Described as "the worst three miles in the State of Montana," the road was a quagmire most of the year. The more adventurous guests toured the park by horse or on foot, staying at backcountry chalets built by the Great Northern Railway an easy day's horseback ride apart.

As automobiles became more common, Glacier's first superintendent, Major William R. Logan, began to study the possibility of a trans-mountain road that would open the interior of the park to visitors. With a suitable route finally chosen, work began in 1922 on the section of road from Apgar to Avalanche Creek. The following year work began on the eastern side of the park to connect St. Mary Chalets with Going-to-the-Sun Chalets.

The twelve-mile alpine section of the Trans-Mountain Highway would prove to be incredibly difficult. Work began in 1925. Bridges, tunnels, arches and retaining walls had to be constructed and a three-mile section blasted from the nearly vertical cliffs of the Garden Wall. Construction crews often had to dangle from ropes hundreds of feet above the ground. Crews working with blasting powder wore heavy wool socks over their hobnailed boots to prevent sparks from setting off a potentially catastrophic explosion. Rockslides, brutal weather, and bears that raided the work-men's food supplies were a constant danger. Despite precautions, three men lost their lives during the road's construction, two from falls and a third who was struck by a large rock.

On July 15, 1933, the narrow gravel road officially opened to traffic. Chili, hot dogs and coffee were served to over 4,000 people who attended the ceremony, including representatives of the Blackfeet, Flathead and Kootenai tribes. During the dedication, the Trans-Mountain Road was officially named "Going-to-the-Sun Road." According to legend, the Blackfeet demi-god Napi, also known as Old Man or Sour Spirit, son of Sun and Moon, came down from the Sun in a time of great need to teach his people to hunt with bow and arrow, how to drive buffalo into an enclosure where they could be killed, how to tan hides and build tipis. After his work was done, he climbed back to the Sun, leaving the image of his face on nearby Going-to-the-Sun Mountain (*Glacier National Park: Its Trails and Treasures*, Mathilde Edith Holtz and Katharine Isabel Bemis, 1917).

The construction of Going-to-the-Sun Road is still considered the most difficult and dangerous civil engineering project in U.S. history. The road was designated a National Civil Engineering Landmark as well as a National Historic Landmark. It is also listed on the National Register of Historic Places.

Engineering marvel though the road undoubtedly is, I couldn't help but breathe a sigh of relief when the pilot car eventually appeared to lead us past the construction zone. Cautiously, wary of the loose gravel and slick bare rock, we followed the line of cars until we were once again safely on the pavement. When Upper St. Mary Lake finally appeared in the distance, I pulled gratefully into the Wild Goose Island overlook where I could work the cramps out of my hands. Going-to-the-Sun Road is definitely not for those with a fear of heights!

The lake had faded to a dull pewter color in the flat light, and a few sleet pellets rattled against the windshield. My friend Pat, who'd flown up from the hot, steamy Texas Gulf Coast to join me, grabbed her camera and bravely ducked out of the car, determined to get a few photos of the rocky islet. Moments later, she climbed back inside, calmly brushed sleet from her jacket, and we resumed our journey.

The Blackfeet called Upper and Lower St. Mary Lakes the "Walled-in-Lakes" or the "Inside Lakes." The origin of the modern name is uncertain, but is sometimes attributed to Father Pierre De Smet, a Jesuit missionary of the 1840s. Others believe the lakes were named by mountain man Hugh Monroe (known to the Blackfeet as Rising Wolf), or by members of the Boundary Survey crew of 1870. Regardless of how the lakes got their name, Upper St. Mary Lake is a favorite with photographers, and picturesque Wild Goose Island in the middle of the lake provides the setting for a touching legend. As the Red Bus drivers tell it, a young brave swam out to the island one day and met a beautiful maiden from a different tribe. They promptly fell in love. When their elders found out, they were outraged and decided to separate them. The Great Spirit took pity on the devoted lovers and changed them into two wild geese that flew away, never to be separated again.

The Blackfeet name for the island is *Natosapi,* or Holy Person Island. It may have been the setting for "The Two Brothers," a Blackfeet legend recounted by Walter McClintock in *The Old North Trail* (1910).

There were once two brothers, Nopatsis, the elder, and Akaiyan, the younger. Nopatsis was married to a thoroughly evil woman, who lusted for Akaiyan and wanted to see the younger brother ruined. This shrew of a wife pestered Nopatsis day and night to send his brother away. At the same time, she made seductive advances toward Akaiyan.

She then resorted to the most evil and wretched thing she could do.

One day when Nopatsis returned home, he found his wife with her clothing ripped and her hair in a mess. The wife told him that Akaiyan had tried to have his way with her. Nopatsis was livid and sickened by this report. He then resolved to do away with his brother.

Every summer the waterfowl molt, leaving thousands of feathers on the surface of the lakes. The people gather the small feathers to make fletching for their arrows. It so happened that Nopatsis lived on the shores of such a lake, and it was only natural for the two brothers to gather the feathers together. Nopatsis and Akaiyan went out in a buffalo-hide boat to an island in the middle of the lake, far from shore, where the feathers were usually quite dense.

While Akaiyan was busy gathering feathers, Nopatsis left him to die on the island. This lake was deep, prone to sudden storms, and the island was too far from the mainland for a person to leave without a boat. Thus it was pointless for Akaiyan to try swimming home. As Akaiyan looked toward home, he saw Nopatsis jeering and uttering curses at him. Nopatsis repeated the terrible lie that his wife had told him, shouting it across the lake. Akaiyan cried out that he was innocent, but it was now too late.

Deeply hurt, Akaiyan looked into the water and began to cry. He prayed to the nature spirits to help him. He called to the Sun and the Moon to vindicate him. Then he built himself a shelter made of branches and a bed made of feathers. He learned how to make clothing for himself from the skins of ducks and geese, taming some of them and feeding them in order to have food for the winter. He lived in this way for many months.

One day a little beaver came and invited Akaiyan to visit

his family's den. Akaiyan was by now very lonely, and gladly accepted. When he entered the lodge, the Great Beaver, so old that his fur was white, treated Akaiyan as an honored guest, asking how he came to be living on the island. Akaiyan then told the story of his wicked sister in law. The great Beaver was outraged by the injustice done to Akaiyan and vowed to do whatever he could on behalf of this innocent young man. At the gracious invitation of the beavers, Akaiyan spent the winter in the warmth of their lodge, learning all the medicine and magic of the beavers.

As summer returned, the Great Beaver asked Akaiyan what gift he would like to take with him. Akaiyan responded that he would like to take his host's youngest son as a companion. The Great Beaver was reluctant to grant this, as this son was his favorite. But at last the Great Beaver agreed, also giving Akaiyan instructions for building a sacred beaver lodge when he returned to his home village on the mainland. The knowledge of the Great Beaver had such powerful magic that Akaiyan now had supernatural powers on his side. There was nothing more for him to fear, whether on the island or at home on the mainland.

In several months, Nopatsis returned to the island, expecting to find the bones of Akaiyan, who had long been given up for dead. While Nopatsis was busy looking around, Akaiyan carried the little beaver in his arms and then got into Nopatsis's boat, which he took to the mainland. The roles were reversed; it was now Nopatsis who pleaded with his brother across the water.

On his return to the mainland, Akaiyan was well received by the people of the beaver lodge. As the Great Beaver had instructed, Akaiyan built a sacred beaver lodge and taught the people the dances and chants of the beaver.

After this had been accomplished, Akaiyan returned to

the island to bring the little beaver back to his family. He also found the bones of Nopatsis and buried them. The Great Beaver was so pleased that Akaiyan had returned his son that he gave him the sacred peace pipe as a sign of his gratitude.

Tempted to swim in this beautiful lake? The waters are deep and cold, barely warming to fifty degrees even in summer! The lake is also prone to sudden strong winds that make kayaking or canoeing on the lake dangerous. The most violent winds are called "Kootenai winds" by the Blackfeet, and waves can reach twice the height of a man. According to legend, the winds are caused by an enormous moose. Mark Daniels, then General Superintendant of National Parks, related the legend to the *San Antonio Light* on October 24, 1915:

One time a young brave left the protecting circle of a teepee to hunt moose in the great St. Mary canyon. Upon arriving at the head of St. Mary's lake he spied in the distance a moose of enormous size. He drew his bow but before he could let fly the shaft, the moose flapped his ears, causing a wind of such intensity that it blew the brave prone to the ground. At each attempt to rise, the moose flapped his gigantic ears until the canyon was filled with winds that blew the lake almost on end. Since that time, the presiding god of the wind in this canyon has been the phantom moose.

As Going-to-the-Sun Road descends toward the St. Mary Valley, evergreen forests are replaced by aspens and open grasslands that are better adapted to the drier and windier conditions on the east side of the mountains. For hundreds of years, Native Americans hunted the buffalo that roamed the meadows at the foot of Upper St. Mary Lake. By the late 1800s the buffalo were gone, and with them, a nomadic way of life that had lasted for thousands of years.

Development soon followed. In 1912, the Great Northern Railway built St. Mary Chalets at the lower end of the lake. The opening of Going-to-the-Sun Road in 1933 brought many more visitors to the area and in 1932, former ranger Hugh Black and his wife Margaret built a small resort at St. Mary, a few hundred yards from the east entrance to Going-to-the-Sun Road. Over the years, the resort was enlarged and renovated several times. St. Mary Lodge and Resort is now owned by Glacier Park Inc. and offers accommodations in rustic cabins, a motel, and the main lodge.

The community of St. Mary has only about fifty year-round residents, but during the warmer months, when Going-to-the-Sun Road is open, hundreds of visitors drive past St. Mary Lodge and Resort each day. Many of them stop to enjoy lunch or to sample the gourmet fudge in the lodge's enormous gift shop. Probably few of them suspect that St. Mary Lodge, like many other historic hotels, has a few "non-paying" guests.

Jerry Black, grandson of Hugh and Margaret Black, had told me on a previous visit that "things sometimes got interesting in the fall." Men's voices and the sounds of people moving around would occasionally be reported by employees getting the lodge ready to close for the winter.

"People think they hear someone walking, especially down in the basement," Black said, "but you know there can't be anyone there, because there are only three people left and you know where the other two are."

A mischievous spirit is also reported to haunt the gift shop. "A lot of things happen here at night," manager Athena Chakeres told us. "There are twenty thousand items on the shelves, and we make sure everything's in its place at closing. When we come in the next morning, we'll find a little bear or something on the floor. Sometimes my dream catchers will be out of their boxes. I find stuff in all sorts of obscure places. Sometimes keys will be moved. One night a Christmas ornament flew off the tree and landed on a different display."

No one knows who moves things around in the gift shop, but for hundreds of years, Native Americans, trappers, and mountain men roamed the trails of the St. Mary Valley. Perhaps they return in spirit from time to time, to explore the area they once knew so well.

One of them may have been seen not far from the lodge. According to Jerry Black, "There's an old grizzled guy who's been seen walking back out of Going-to-the-Sun Road by visitor center personnel at St. Mary. They thought he looked rather strange, so they turned back for another look and he was gone. It happened once or twice a year, late at night just before they shut down. He never did anything. His clothing was definitely dated and he had quite a beard. He looked like he'd been out in the woods for a while."

It's tempting to speculate that the grizzled figure may be the spirit of Hugh Monroe, Rising Wolf. Monroe was born in Quebec in 1798 and joined the Hudson's Bay Company in 1814. Assigned as an interpreter to the Piegans, one of the tribes of the Blackfeet confederacy, Monroe eventually married the chief's daughter. The free-ranging life of a hunter and trapper suited him, and he spent the rest of his long life with the Blackfeet.

As a young man, Monroe camped with the Blackfeet near the Inside Lakes, now Upper and Lower St Mary Lakes. Later, he hunted and trapped the abundant game in the area, accompanying the Blackfeet on perilous treks into the mountains. When he died at the age of ninety-eight, he was buried near a buffalo jump that overlooks the Two Medicine River.

Shortly before his death in 1896, Monroe recounted his adventures to James Willard Schultz, author of *Blackfeet Tales of Glacier National Park*. Years later, Schultz, who himself had lived for many years among the Blackfeet, wrote *Rising Wolf, the White*

Blackfeet, and described Monroe as a "bearded old man, honored by all who knew him."

If the grizzled old mountain man reportedly seen by visitor center personnel was indeed the spirit of Hugh Monroe, I wonder what he thinks of Going-to-the-Sun Road and the hundreds of vehicles that cross Glacier Park in little more than one hour!

LAKE MCDONALD LODGE

Picture yourself standing at the bow of a wooden launch as it glides across the dark glassy waters of 472-foot-deep Lake McDonald. It's a cool, misty June morning in 1914. You and your family arrived at Belton by train the previous night, en route to John Lewis's newly-opened Lewis Glacier Hotel. The hotel is not yet reachable by road, so you and other guests took a wagon from Belton Chalet to Apgar Village, where everyone boarded the launch Cassie D *for the scenic voyage to the hotel. You and your family plan to spend the summer hiking, fishing, and boating. You might even try a quick dip in the lake, although swimming isn't advised. Carved out by glaciers thousands of years ago, the ten-mile-long lake is fed almost entirely by melting snow and is very cold, even in midsummer.*

As your launch approaches the dock, you can just make out the roofline of the Lewis Glacier Hotel above the mist. Constructed on the site of an earlier hotel built in 1895 by wealthy furrier James Snyder, Lewis's impressive new hotel with its balconies and scrollwork closely resembles the great lodges built by the Great Northern Railway. You stroll up from the dock and enter a soaring three-story lobby decorated with Chinese lanterns and a huge stone fireplace carved with Native American symbols. Unlike the larger lodges built by the Great Northern Railway, this hotel has a hunting lodge atmosphere with Lewis's trophies displayed on the walls. You settle contentedly into one of the arts-and-crafts chairs and wait for the porters to bring your trunks up from the boat. This, you are suddenly sure, will be a very good summer.

Fast forward nearly a century: Lewis's Glacier Hotel, now Lake McDonald Lodge, is still a popular destination for park visitors. The lobby looks much the same as it did in 1914, but since the opening of Going-to-the-Sun Road in 1933, most guests arrive by automobile and the former back entry now serves as the hotel's main entrance. A broad flight of stairs leads up from the dock to the original front door. Although the launch no longer brings guests from Apgar, tourists can enjoy scenic tours of the lake aboard the historic vessel *DeSmet* on fine summer days. Built in 1930, the *DeSmet* gives tourists an authentic glimpse of the old days when the hotel was accessible only by water.

Despite the multi-story lobby, the Lake McDonald Lodge feels more like a comfortable private residence than the other great park lodges do. It's easy to imagine Lewis's friend and neighbor, cowboy artist Charlie Russell, spinning yarns beside the massive fireplace in the evenings to amuse Lewis's guests. During the catastrophic flood of 1964, however, the tranquil atmosphere of this most homelike of lodges must have been charged with fear. Days of heavy rain caused the rapid melting of an unusually deep winter's snowpack. Lake McDonald rose so swiftly that Upper McDonald Creek reversed its flow and sent torrents of muddy water swirling through the hotel's kitchen and dining room. Damage to the main lodge was averted when a logjam on Snyder Creek was dynamited, but roads, bridges, and trails throughout the park were destroyed.

Despite the seasonal risks of floods and forest fires, Lake McDonald Lodge, like all the park's lodges, has a devoted following. Many guests return year after year, to hike, fish, boat, or simply enjoy the magnificent scenery. Perhaps guests from long ago have also returned at times, to roam once more the lodge they loved so much in life. If so, their gentle spirits left no report of their comings and goings. For many years, Lake McDonald Lodge was the only park lodge without a ghost story of its own.

Until, that is, Robert Lucke decided to take a hand.

"Robbie" Lucke is a legend among "gear jammers," as the drivers of Glacier's Red Buses are called. A veteran newspaper reporter who has spent nine summers at Glacier, Lucke wrote the training manual for new bus drivers. Much to their delight, Lucke included many of the ghost stories he'd heard from other employees of Glacier Park Inc. He'd noticed that children on long tours quickly grew bored with stories about the history of the park, no matter how skillfully told. As a newspaperman, Lucke knew that most people love ghost stories, so he decided to entertain the youngsters with eerie tales about the great lodges. The experiment was wildly successful: the kids were enthralled, their parents appreciative, and the tips generous.

Although Lake McDonald Lodge may have lacked a resident spirit of its own, Lucke did have a number of odd experiences while driving back to the lodge from other places. Here, with his generous permission, are three excerpts from an article he wrote called "Ghosts in Glacier's Grandest."

> As a driver of Red Bus 93, several times when deadheading back to the hotel later in the afternoon from another point, I have looked back through the rear view mirror and just got an instant glimpse of a bus full of smiling and chatting customers dressed much different than today's guests. So many times has that happened to me that when deadheading back to Lake McDonald from another hotel, when going through the entrance gate, I will tell the entrance ranger that I am hauling the ghosts of one lodge who want to visit the ghosts in another lodge.

In 2006, location manager Todd Ashcraft decided to offer daily tours at the hotel. Hotel tours had proven to be popular at Many Glacier Hotel, but Ashcraft wanted something out of the ordinary for Lake McDonald Lodge. Lucke, recalling his own eerie experiences, suggested a "ghost" that would appear on cue, cross a balcony, and disappear back into the hotel, giving unsuspecting tourists a thrill.

What resulted was a mixture of high drama and Keystone Kops. As Lucke wrote,

> Bellmen doing hotel walking tours and interested in tips from excited guests have frequently taken to dressing unsuspecting porters in sheets and having them float down the third floor balcony at opportune moments. This has been effective in more ways than might be suspected, especially when porters had to put their sheet on so quickly that they did not cut eye holes in it and in the midst of effective moans and groans, ran right into upright posts and fell to the ground amid real moans and groans.

Their efforts to provide visitors with a spooky experience may have lasted only one season, but there's an unexpected twist to the tale. As Lucke later wrote:

> During the summer of 2008, a woman dressed in old time clothes was seen by a security man and night auditor many times looking out the lobby windows that open to the lakeside verandah. Many times night people would hear loud arguing coming from the balconies like guests were fighting but there were never any guests fighting at all and no complaints ever from guests about the loud arguing. One night a lady auditor felt something run its fingers through her hair. It was not scary at all, she reported, but comforting. Whether or not I inadvertently hauled those ghosts from another location to Lake McDonald or they were always there and there were just people more in tune to feel their presence, I do not know. I do know that for those

who saw the ghosts at Lake McDonald Lodge the summer
of 2008, they were as real as the bellmen stoking the lobby
fireplace or a dining room server during the breakfast rush.

Had Lake McDonald Lodge finally managed to attract a ghost
of its own? Pat and I decided to find out. We arrived at noon on
a misty September morning to find a big tour coach and several
Red Buses unloading passengers at the door. There was already
a long line for lunch at Russell's Fireside Dining Room, with its
paneled walls and hunting trophies, so we opted for a quick lunch
in the aptly-named Lucke's Lounge.

The bartender had worked at the lodge only for a few weeks
and hadn't heard of any ghost stories. Eager to help, he suggested
that we talk to Phil, the maintenance manager, who was also the
lodge's winter caretaker. If anyone knew any stories, the bartender
assured us, it would be the winter keeper.

We finally tracked Phil to the registration desk, where he'd just
finished replacing one of the ceiling lights. He didn't recall any
unusual encounters at Lake McDonald Lodge. "Tools go missing
sometimes," he said, "but I just misplace them. I did hear a story
from old-timers years ago. I don't know if it's true, but they told
me about a cook, Maude, who worked here for a long time. She
was world famous for her beef stroganoff. They said that when
she died, her ashes were spread in the lake and around the lodge.
People who'd been caretakers in the winter used to claim they
would get a very uncomfortable feeling just before they would
smell beef stroganoff. If it ever happened to me, the old-timers
told me to just say 'Now Maude, knock it off, I'm okay,' and
it would go away. Supposedly you can smell it anywhere on the
entire facility, mostly in the lodge."

"Have you ever smelled it?" I asked curiously. Phantom odors
are often reported in haunted places. Oddly enough, sometimes
only one or two people in a group can smell them, although to

those who can, the odors are very real.

Phil shook his head. "There is an odd smell in Room 67 at the Village Inn though. Every time I get a call from the inn, it's about Room 66 or 67. You should go down to Apgar and talk to the housekeeping staff. Some of them have been there for years. They know all the stories."

We thanked Phil and made a note to drive down to Apgar the following day. The lobby was beginning to empty as the tour groups left, so we took the opportunity to sit down for a few minutes in front of the six-foot-high masonry fireplace carved with Native American pictographs, some say by artist Charlie Russell. Flames flickered among the five-foot long logs on the hearth, and it was very easy to relax and imagine ourselves back in the old days, listening to Charlie spin tall tales for Lewis's guests.

To our disappointment, the lodge itself was fully booked that night, but we managed to reserve one of the rustic log cabins overlooking the lake. The cabins had been built around 1907, before the present Lake McDonald Lodge was constructed, and predate the establishment of Glacier National Park itself. Our cabin was 2A, a side-by-side duplex with a small porch that reminded me of the cozy tourist cabins I'd stayed in as a child in the 1950s. We unlocked the door and stepped into a foul odor so strong that I nearly choked.

"Open the windows!" I gasped. Pat gave me a puzzled look, but helpfully began to open all the windows. I propped the door open for a few minutes. Perhaps the cabin would air out while we went down to the shore to get a few photos.

Lake McDonald was calm, with a few spreading ripples wherever fish rose to the surface. The *DeSmet* bobbed gently at the dock while her crew finished preparing her for a cruise around the lake. We strolled along the beach, idly looking for a place where the Kootenai Indians might have danced. The Kootenai, who roamed the west side of what is now Glacier Park, called the lake

"Sacred Dancing Place," and are said to have held dances and ceremonies along the shore. A nearby waterfall on McDonald Creek is called Sacred Dancing Falls in remembrance of those days.

After a leisurely dinner in the Fireside Restaurant, we returned to our cabin, hoping that the stench would be gone, but it was just as strong as it had been hours earlier. The outdoor temperature was still mild, so we decided to leave the windows open when we went to bed.

During the night, I was jolted awake by a sharp "CRACK!" from overhead. Old wooden beams sometimes creak in cold or windy weather, but it was only mid-September, and there was no wind. For a moment I wondered whether I might have heard a gunshot from the nearby woods, but there is, of course, no hunting in the park. Whatever the cause, Pat never stirred. I listened intently for other noises, but I heard no further sounds from inside or outside the cabin. Eventually I fell asleep.

When we got up in the morning, Pat discovered that her books had been swept off the table where she'd placed them and were lying in a heap on the floor. Like me, she'd been awakened during the night by a noise. This time, however, it was the sound of footsteps walking around her bed. At first she thought I must have gotten up, but I was asleep. She estimated that the footsteps continued for almost a minute before fading away. She hadn't heard the loud crack that had awakened me.

While we were comparing notes, I realized that the foul odor I assumed had been caused by bathroom drains had dissipated. Much to my astonishment, Pat told me that *she hadn't smelled the odor at all.* That explained the odd look she'd given me before she'd begun opening windows.

That left us scratching our heads. Phil had told us about the odor of beef stroganoff just before we walked over to the cabin. Had that somehow "programmed" me to smell something that wasn't really there? Or was this an example of a psychic odor, one that not everyone can smell? And what—or who—caused the loud crack during the night, and the footsteps, and swept Pat's books onto the floor?

We sought Phil out after breakfast, finding him in the dining room. As the long-time maintenance manager for the lodge, he might shed some light on what had happened. Although he listened closely to our account, he could offer no explanation. The cabin had been built more than a century ago, and no doubt thousands of people had stayed in it over the years. Our strange experience would remain a mystery.

Lake McDonald Lodge also featured, at least marginally, in another unsolved mystery: the disappearance of two young men in 1924. On August 24, brothers Joseph and William Whitehead left Granite Park Chalet on a twenty-mile hike to the Lewis Glacier Hotel, now Lake McDonald Lodge. They never made it. Somewhere on the trail between Granite Park Chalet and the Lewis Glacier Hotel, they vanished.

When they did not return home to Chicago as planned, their mother requested that a search be made for them. Search parties were sent out to cover all the likely routes the brothers might have taken. The weeks-long search was intently followed by readers of newspapers across the country and eventually involved J. Edgar Hoover's Bureau of Investigation. Even President Calvin Coolidge expressed an interest. No trace of the young men was found, and the search was called off on September 17.

A few days later, a report by three riders employed by the Park Saddle Horse Company surfaced. On August 24 they claimed to have met two young men on the trail halfway between Granite Park Chalet and the Lewis Glacier Hotel. That was the last known sighting of the Whiteheads, if the two men had indeed been the brothers. Rumors ran wild: they had been attacked by a bear, fallen over a cliff or into a crevasse, had gotten lost, been kidnapped or murdered. No evidence was ever found to support the rumors.

Many years later an elderly woman whose husband had been close to the investigation in the 1920s told seasonal ranger Doug Follett that the Whitehead brothers had been robbed and murdered. According to her, their bodies had been wrapped in barbed wire, weighted with rocks and sunk in Lake Five near Whitefish. Unless a sonar-equipped boat someday discovers two skeletons wrapped in barbed wire on the bottom of Lake Five, the disappearance of the Whitehead brothers is likely to remain Glacier's greatest unsolved mystery.

Pat and I checked out of our cabin the next morning, already looking forward to next year's visit. Before we left, however, we met with Todd Ashcraft, the lodge's innovative location manager. He was supervising preparations for the approaching end of the season. There were, he explained, certain traditions that were observed on opening day and closing day.

"On the morning of opening, usually May 20th or 21st," he told us, "everybody gathers down at the lake. We have a log down there and we bring it up the stairs and into the hotel in a procession. Then we have a little ceremony and light the fire. Usually the fire stays lit [all summer] until we throw the last log back in the lake. The only times when the fire is allowed to go out is if we have a bad fire year and are not allowed to burn anything.

"On the morning of closing, usually the 26th of September, I gather all the employees and guests, and Mr. Lucke thanks each department for their hard work over the summer and tells the guests a little bit about what went on. As the last log burns in the fireplace, the three bellmen grab it safely—hopefully—and go through the middle of the hotel. We carry fire extinguishers behind them. They head out the back doors with the guests and employees following, and go down the steps and start running with the log and jump off the dock into the water. That's the end of the season for us. The bellmen are dreading it because they have to jump in the lake and it is very cold."

The closing ceremony sounds like great fun. One thing seems certain—the crowd of cheering spectators will probably be larger than can be seen.

THE MANY GHOSTS OF MANY GLACIER HOTEL

IMAGINE WHAT IT WOULD IT BE LIKE TO SPEND SIX MONTHS ALONE at a boarded-up hotel in remote wilderness twelve miles from the nearest human company at Babb—if you could even get there through the drifts that usually clog the narrow, winding road. That's why only those who are tough, resourceful and able to tolerate isolation for months at a time become winter caretakers at Many Glacier Hotel. Each day brings a struggle through 400 yards of deep snow between the caretaker's cottage and the hotel. The half-mile-long, dimly-lit wooden building must be inspected, and the fine snow that has blown in through chinks shoveled out. Once a week, over two hundred rooms must be checked for damage, and repairs made if needed. The only sounds are the shriek of the wind, the hiss of snow, and the occasional howl of a coyote.

It sounds like a perfect setting for a horror film, and indeed, legend has it that the film *The Shining*, based on Stephen King's novel was filmed at Many Glacier Hotel. In fact, the exterior and interior shots are of Colorado's famously haunted Stanley Hotel. Only the opening scene, an aerial shot of a mountain road, was filmed in Glacier National Park.

Many Glacier Hotel is the grandest and most remote of the hotels built by the Great Northern Railway. The rambling structure has welcomed tens of thousands of guests since it opened on July 4, 1915. At first, guests arrived by horse from the backcountry chalets. The comforts offered by the big hotel must have been very welcome after days in the saddle, and the hotel's location on the shores of Swiftcurrent Lake (then called McDermott Lake) offered spectacular views of the surrounding mountains.

Over the years, "Many," as the hotel is affectionately called by employees and guests, has survived several close brushes with disaster. A raging forest fire in 1936 nearly claimed the structure, while in 1964, 1975 and 2006, Swiftcurrent Lake flooded, cutting off the road to Babb and sending torrents of icy water into the building's lower level. Nonetheless, the hotel has a devoted following among its employees and guests. Some come to marvel at its Swiss-chalet style architecture. Others come to hike, fish, ride, or photograph wildlife, returning at dusk to enjoy a good dinner and a comfortable bed.

Many guests return year after year, drawn by the incredible beauty of the surroundings and the hotel's quirky charm. Apparently some of them loved this idyllic spot so much in life that they may have returned after death. It is said that their peaceful spirits are felt or even seen at times by those who are sensitive enough.

My friend Pat and I arrived just before dusk on a cool evening in early September. The jagged peaks on the far side of Swiftcurrent Lake stood out starkly against the sun's afterglow, and the Swiss chalet–style hotel was already shrouded by deepening shadows. I left Pat and our luggage with one of the attentive bellmen and then drove up the hill to park in the lot overlooking the hotel.

The bellman had told us that bears sometimes strolled through the property after dark, so I hastily followed other late-arriving guests down the steep stone stairway that led back to the hotel's entrance. I'd had a close encounter with a bear on my first visit to Many Glacier forty years earlier and had no desire to repeat the experience. My husband and I had arrived at twilight and, eager to hike around Swiftcurrent Lake before dark, I'd left him unpacking our suitcases and set off on the 2.4-mile trail alone. Near the outlet of the lake, the trail crossed a boggy area with head-high reeds that limited visibility on all sides. I squelched resolutely onward, feeling as if I'd been plunged into a green world miles from anywhere.

Suddenly I smelled the strong odor of what I thought was wet dog. I paused, listening. Nothing moved. By then it was beginning to get dark, so I hurried on, determined to get back to the hotel while I could still see my way. When I mentioned the wet dog smell to the desk clerk, he told me that was the characteristic odor of black bears! Although it never showed itself or made any noise, the bear had to have been very close.

In 1967, just four years before my experience, two young women had been killed and a man seriously injured by grizzlies in the park. One of the attacks had happened at Many Glacier Campground, down the road from the hotel. I'd even read Jack Olson's book about the tragedy, *The Night of the Grizzlies*, published in 1969. Yet in my haste to get in a hike before sundown, I'd ignored several of the basic safety precautions when hiking in bear country: don't hike alone; make lots of noise; carry bear spray; and be aware that bears are most active at dawn and dusk.

I never hiked that trail—or any other—at twilight again.

This time, there was no sign of bears. I hurried inside, slightly out of breath, to find Pat waiting for me near the front desk with our luggage and the bellman. He was eager to relate a story told to him by the previous winter caretaker. One day the caretaker had fought his way from his cottage to the hotel through a howling blizzard. Once there, he meticulously checked each of the rooms in the cavernous building and decided to do some routine maintenance on the third floor. It was bitterly cold inside the room, and after working a while he decided to take a coffee break to warm up. He had just finished his coffee when suddenly he heard a tremendous crash. The noise seemed to come from a nearby room, so he set down his mug and hurried down the corridor expecting to find a window blown in by fierce winds. He found nothing. Puzzled and uneasy for no apparent reason, he decided to quit for the day.

The next morning the wind moderated and he returned to the hotel. When he entered the dim, cavernous lobby, he caught a whiff of fresh coffee. There, on a counter, was his favorite mug— still steaming.

We thanked the bellman for sharing his friend's eerie story and went in search of supper. Fortunately, we were in time for dinner in the baronial Ptarmigan Restaurant, where banners from each of the Swiss cantons were displayed. The view looking across Swiftcurrent Lake toward massive Grinnell Point was awe-inspiring and dinner was excellent. In quiet moments it was easy to imagine the room as it must have been in the distant past, full of the excited chatter of the "young things" of the 1920s. If echoes from those times still lingered anywhere in the grand old hotel, I thought the Ptarmigan Restaurant was a likely location.

After dinner that evening a log fire was lit in the cavernous main lobby, and guests quietly drifted in to settle in comfortable chairs around the huge hooded fireplace. Many of the guests still wore hiking shorts and boots and had obviously just come in off the trails. A drowsy silence descended on all of us, broken only by the crackle of the flames and an occasional pop as a pine knot burst. It wouldn't have taken much imagination to see shadowy figures in old-fashioned clothing lingering nearby, enjoying the peaceful scene with us.

Almost regretfully we left to go up to our room, which was set into an angle of a wall and overlooked the stairs to the parking lot with mountains visible in the distance. It was rustic but comfortable, and more spacious than we had expected. I opened the windows to allow cool evening air to enter and noted that guests strolling beneath our second-floor windows could be heard as plainly as if they were in our room, and that both the door and the wooden floors squeaked loudly.

The natural creaks and groans of an old building might account for some of the ghost stories we had heard about the hotel, but it certainly couldn't explain the figure of a lady in a red dress seen in his room by a nine-year-old Great Falls boy. The furniture could be plainly seen through the ghost. Startled, the youngster woke up his brother, but the ghost faded away before the other boy saw it.

Then there are the noisy parties in Room 308 in the Annex Building. Guests in adjacent rooms have sometimes called down to the front desk to complain about a loud party in Room 308—even when employees know that it's unoccupied. Once in a while the housekeeping staff will receive a phone call from someone in Room 308, asking for more towels to be brought up. When the maid arrives with an armload of towels, she finds the room empty, with no sign of current occupancy. The Annex was built in 1917 and its rooms were often booked by wealthy families who spent the summer at Many Glacier. Perhaps some of them return now and then to relive happy times.

Pat and I were undisturbed that night, and next morning had breakfast in the Ptarmigan Restaurant overlooking Swiftcurrent Lake, its waters black and glassy, unruffled as yet by any breeze. Our waitress had previously worked in housekeeping and told us that some of the staff felt uneasy while working in the rooms on the lower level.

A gift shop employee also felt that the lower level was creepy at times. She'd had the same room on the lower level for eight years. "Sometimes I'll hear a half-ring on my phone during the night," she said. "No one is ever on the line when I answer." And someone—or something—occasionally taps twice on her door. The first few times it happened she got up and went to the door, but no one was there.

"It's a linoleum floor so you hear everything," she said. "You never hear anyone moving off, so if it's not a ghost, it would have to be someone in stocking feet." She no longer answers the door at night.

The ghost apparently doesn't like being talked about. "I guess he got mad at me," she continued, "because when I came into the store one morning a glass shelf was on the floor. Usually a shelf falls because the brackets give way, but they were still in place. The shelf wasn't broken, but several items that had been on it did break, and one mug with a handle rolled from the shelving unit all the way to the showcase. A couple of kids who lived upstairs knew about the ghost and when they heard the crash they came out of their room right away. They didn't see anyone running away from the shop."

One night she had an even more unusual experience while lying in bed. "I was lying there one night and felt my bed go down. I'd felt that before and just flapped my blanket at it, thinking it was a critter of some sort. This time I looked and saw a butt imprint as if someone had sat down on the bed."

Other guests have also felt an unseen "critter" walk across their beds. In September 2012, first-time guests Justine and her husband checked in to the hotel after a day's hiking. They were given Room 138 on the main floor. Tired and sore, they went to bed early. During the night, Justine was awakened by "a light amount of pressure on the right side of the bed, and a second or two later, at the top of the bed. My husband was happily snoring away, so I know it was not him. I have cats at home, and this felt like pressure from a small cat. A couple hours later, I felt pressure on the right side of the bed again. The pressure was a bit harder. Again, my husband was sound asleep in the other bed. I fell back asleep without any further incidents."

It's when the tourist season winds down, however, that the grand old hotel really seems to come alive.

Jason Wilmot and Kate Richardson spent the winter of 2000-

2001 at Many Glacier. "We stayed in the caretakers' cabin, which is about four hundred yards away from the hotel," Wilmot told me. "It's a world away in a blizzard. We were about seven miles in from the park boundary gate. We went in and out a little bit to Babb, but stayed mostly in. The road was not plowed, and while some of it was often free of snow due to wind, there was a huge drift at the Swiftcurrent dam making driving in impossible. It is very quiet in Many Glacier in winter, and besides our friends and the occasional hotel employee, no park visitors came into the valley for three and a half months."

Their job included checking each of over two hundred rooms in the huge building every day. They soon discovered that the atmosphere in some rooms, particularly those in the basement, made them uneasy. Eventually they decided to check the rooms together—just in case.

Although hotel employees had told them about some of their eerie experiences, nothing really unusual occurred until a big snowstorm hit the area.

"No one had been in or out of the valley for about a week," Wilmot recalled. "In the middle of a heavy wind and snowstorm we went into the hotel to hear piano music playing. Of course, we looked all around to find the source, and found one of those tourist-shop display machines that plays nature music, loon [call]s, and piano music to sell tapes, and it was plugged in and playing music. There may have been a power surge due to the storm. After unplugging it and going on our patrol of the hotel, which was a creepy endeavor when the power was not on throughout most of the hotel, a fire alarm went off right over my head for no reason I can think of other than strong winds and a power surge—or something else. We bugged out of there for the day."

The late Steve Lautenbach, who spent more winters at Many Glacier than any other caretaker, also had his share of adventures. Lautenbach, a New Yorker whose love for the wilderness was obvious in newspaper interviews, spent six months each winter from 2005 to 2008 isolated from civilization, cleaning, remodeling, shoveling snow and chopping wood. In his spare time, he would ski or ice fish on frozen Swiftcurrent Lake. If the weather was bad, he would run to keep in shape through the empty corridors of the half-mile-long building.

Lautenbach knew about the hotel's ghosts before he took the job as caretaker, but he wasn't particularly worried. He didn't believe in ghosts, and the old wooden hotel naturally creaked and groaned a lot, especially on nights when the wind howled around the eves like a lost soul. Still, that couldn't explain the scent of a lady's perfume, or the ghost of a man in a top hat.

One experience did shake his skepticism, however. It happened during his first winter at the hotel. While making his rounds one day, he found an empty wine bottle in the middle of a hallway. It hadn't been there the previous week. He carried the bottle to the locked wine case just outside the dining room. The glass doors were open and there was an empty slot on the rack. He called a friend at Apgar Village, who remembers how upset he was. "He told me he kind of panicked, thinking someone was hanging out there, so he took keys and made his rounds and didn't find anyone. There were no tracks in the snow except his, either. He said, 'I don't believe in ghosts but that was weird!'"

Lautenbach often spoke passionately about the park's grand old lodges. "There's something about them," he would tell reporters. "I just love them. They've got so much character and class."

When reporters asked him if there really were ghosts at Many Glacier, Lautenbach's answer was always the same: "If I say yes, then I'm crazy. If I say no, then I'm a liar."

MYSTERIOUS MARIAS PASS

"THERE IT IS!" PAT EXCLAIMED, POINTING TO THE SIGN NEAR THE top of 5,213-foot Marias Pass. I slowed and turned off Highway 2 at Memorial Square. The parking lot was empty, nearby Summit Campground deserted, the tourists gone. It was late September, and the short alpine summer was over. Although the weather was still mild, with a light breeze and overcast skies, a strong Canadian cold front was barreling down the Rocky Mountain Front and high winds were predicted for the passes. Soon the first early snows would whiten Summit and Calf Robe mountains just to the north. Like Logan Pass on Going-to-the-Sun Road, Marias Pass is noted for extremes of weather, with temperatures falling as low as -55 degrees Fahrenheit in the winter. Deep snow and fierce winds gusting to well over 100 miles per hour can block the pass for days. John F. Stevens, the Great Northern Railway's chief engineer, found that out the hard way when he struggled to the top of the long-sought pass over the Continental Divide during the brutal winter of 1889.

Stevens is credited with the discovery of the pass that eluded several expeditions, but he wasn't the first to set foot on its summit. For centuries, mountain passes such as Cut Bank, Red Eagle, Logan, Piegan, Stoney Indian, Swiftcurrent, Triple Divide, Two Medicine and Marias were used by Native Americans to trade and to raid enemy tribes. The great Blackfeet warrior Running

Eagle is said to have led her war parties westward through Marias Pass, known to the Blackfeet as Bear Pass, Backbone Pass or the Big Gap. The ancient path that follows the Middle Fork of the Flathead River is still called Running Eagle Trail in her memory.

The passes also provided vital access to the buffalo grounds on the plains. Every autumn, when buffalo were fat from a summer of grazing, Salish and Kootenai hunting parties would cross the passes to obtain their winter's supply of meat. In 1812, a Salish hunting party accompanied by two French trappers was spotted by Blackfeet sentries guarding Cut Bank Pass. A huge pile of stones near Cut Bank Pass is said to cover the bodies of those slain in the battle. Legend has it that one old woman was allowed to live, to carry the devastating news back to the Salish.

Marias Pass, the lowest and easiest of the passes to cross, was also the scene of fierce battles. One of those battles took place not far from the site of McCarthysville, a notorious but short-lived boomtown a few miles west of Summit. According to *Glacier National Park* (Holtz, 1917)

> There is an old battlefield of ten acres filled with Indian bones half buried under the mould. The older Blackfeet tell of a struggle between their people and the invading Flatheads. Today the bones of both tribes are lying side-by-side in this field at the head of Bear Creek. The spot can be seen from every Great Northern train crossing the Divide for it lies only five or six hundred yards southeast of the site of old McCarthysville, in the flat just west of skyland.

So many warriors were killed that for years it was said their spirits remained and can be sensed by descendents of those who took part in the battle. Blackfeet tribal member and historian Darrell Norman told me, "Anywhere there has been a battle it's believed you can feel the energies." To this day, there are some who claim to hear the voices of the dead carried by the screaming winds of the pass.

Grace Flandrau, who wrote *The Story of Marias Pass* for the Great Northern Railway in 1925, claimed that the ghost stories were invented by the Blackfeet to keep white men away from the pass. Norman disagreed. "The tales were there long before the white men," he stated with authority.

Haunted or not, Marias Pass has played an important part in opening Glacier National Park to visitors.

In the late 1790s, French and English trappers, traders and missionaries began to explore the Northern Rockies. They were followed by the Lewis and Clark Expedition of 1804-06. Lewis camped within twenty miles of the pass but failed to discover it. He named a nearby river Maria's River after his cousin Maria Wood.. "Marias," now pronounced with a long "i", was later applied by white men to the pass as well.

The first white men known to have crossed the pass were Finan McDonald, Michel Bourdeau, and Baptiste Boucher, employees of the North West Company, a Canadian fur trading company. In July 1810, the three men accompanied a large hunting party of Salish Indians who crossed Marias Pass on their way to the buffalo grounds east of the mountains. They were intercepted by a Blackfeet war party but survived the battle.

Drawn from accounts by early explorers, a map showing the approximate location of Marias Pass was published in 1840. Over the next several decades, various expeditions set out to find the pass, described by Piegan Chief Little Dog as a broad, wide valley with a well-marked trail although somewhat overgrown with brush. Although some of the expeditions actually came within sight of the eastern entrance, for one reason or another the pass continued to evade discovery. It was almost as if Nature itself conspired to hide the pass.

The Great Northern Railway had spent several years looking

for a way to extend its line from Minnesota across the Northern Rockies to Puget Sound. The pass described by Chief Little Dog sounded ideal, relatively low and with an easy grade. The railway company's chief engineer, John F. Stevens, was sent to locate the pass and determine whether it would be suitable for rail traffic. In December of 1889, Stevens and his Flathead guide Koonsa arrived at the pass.

Flandrau describes the scene:

It was December now and the snow was so deep that the small outfit was abandoned and Stevens and his guide set out on improvised snowshoes they themselves had strung with rawhide. It was very cold. When they reached what is known as False Summit, a place some miles east of the pass, the Flathead declared himself unable to proceed and Stevens went on alone. He modestly attributes to mere chance the fact that he walked right into the present Marias Pass and continued by it far enough west to make sure the divide was really crossed and he was in western drainage.

Then he turned back. At the summit he made a bivouac for the night. The deep snow prevented his having a fire; without it he dared not lie down for the extreme cold. Tramping out a runway, he walked back and forth all night to keep from freezing to death. He learned afterwards that at the Agency on the plains the thermometer fell almost to forty below zero; what it was up there on the ridge of the continent, hundreds of feet higher, Mr. Stevens makes no attempt to say.

At daybreak he set out. The Flathead, with what seems the most surprising nonchalance, even for an Indian, had allowed his fire to go out, and he was found by Mr. Stevens almost dead from the cold. They returned together to the Agency on Badger Creek.

Now that the pass had finally been found, construction proceeded swiftly. By 1891, trains were running from Midvale (East Glacier) across the 56-mile Marias Pass to Belton (West Glacier) along the southern edge of what would become Glacier National Park. To commemorate Stevens' feat, the Great Northern Railway placed a statue of him at the top of Marias Pass in 1925.

Motorists could now load their vehicles aboard Great Northern Railway cars and ship them from one side of the mountains to the other. After 1930, when the last segment of U.S. Highway 2 was completed over the pass, motorists had the option of driving the new road instead. The new highway, which ran from Portland, Maine to Portland, Oregon, was known as the Roosevelt International Highway, and a 60-foot-tall obelisk resembling the Washington Monument was constructed on the Continental Divide. The monument honors President Theodore Roosevelt, who considered conservation of natural resources of vital importance.

On a large boulder nearby is a bronze plaque dedicated to the memory of William H. Morrison, an early forest ranger, trapper, and gambler. If it hadn't been for "Slippery Bill," as he was better known, Memorial Square might not exist today.

Morrison worked for the Great Northern Railway in the 1890s. He is said to have earned the name "Slippery Bill" during a poker game one winter in the railroad construction camp at McCarthysville, referred to by one visitor as a "seething Sodom of Wickedness," with twenty saloons, eight houses of ill repute, and two grocery stores. One version of the story says that Morrison won a large amount of money. Knowing that he'd be lucky to escape with his life if he left with his winnings, he pocketed most of the money, casually left the rest on the table, and told his companions that he'd soon be back. He never returned. According to *The Flathead Story* by historian Charlie Shaw, nine bodies belonging to men who apparently lacked Morrison's shrewdness were found the following spring when the snow melted at McCarthysville. .

When the construction camp moved farther west, Morrison obtained "squatter's rights" to 160 acres at Summit, on the top of Marias Pass. He spent the next several years trapping and prospecting. In 1898, Morrison became a seasonal ranger for the Lewis and Clark Forest Reserve, with his headquarters at Summit. The early rangers were experienced backwoodsmen chosen for their toughness, like Albert "Death on the Trail" Reynolds, who boasted that he could walk a horse to death, and Belly River ranger Joe Cosley, a notorious poacher. They led lives of incredible hardship—and wouldn't have had it any other way. In 1915, author Mary Roberts Rinehart wrote of them in *Through Glacier Park*:

> The rangers keep going all winter. There is much to be done. In the summer it is forest fires and outlaws. In the winter there are no forest fires, but there are poachers after mountain sheep and goats, opium smugglers, bad men from over the Canadian border. Now and then a ranger freezes to death. All summer these intrepid men on their sturdy horses go about armed with revolvers. But in the fall—snow begins early in September, sometimes even in August—they take to snowshoes. With a carbine strung to his shoulders, matches in a waterproof case, snowshoes and a package of food in his pocket, the Glacier Park ranger covers unnumbered miles, patrolling the wildest and most storm-ridden country in America. He travels alone. The imprint of a strange snowshoe on the trail rouses his suspicion. Single-handed he follows the marks in the snow. A blizzard comes. He makes a wikiup of branches, lights a small fire, and plays solitaire until the weather clears.

As a forest ranger, Morrison's dedication to duty was somewhat casual. A fellow ranger wrote, "Slippery Bill told me how he would stand in the door of the saloon, gaze at the distant land-scape, return to the shelf where he kept the Government records, and write in his official diary, 'Looking over the Forest.'" He also ran a lively business on the side, selling liquor to train crews and passengers, and periodically rode with them to Essex to pick up mail and supplies.

Little is known of Morrison's early life, but an article in the Kalispell, Montana *Daily Inter Lake* of August 4, 1975, described him as a well-spoken man who quoted Shakespeare and had a sharp tongue on occasion. When the train stopped for water one day, an eastern passenger approached him and asked, "How do people make a living in this windswept, unpleasant, God-forsaken place?" Bill is said to have retorted, "Lady, most of us make a comfortable living by minding our own business."

Morrison was reportedly among the spectators when John F. Stevens, discoverer of Marias Pass, spoke at the dedication of his statue at Summit in 1925. When Stevens vividly described how he almost froze to death in a blizzard at the top of Marias Pass that dreadful night in December 1889, Morrison called out, "Why didn't you come over to my house?" and pointed to his cabin. "I was living right over there."

A few years before he died, Morrison agreed to donate part of his claim to the federal government for the erection of an obelisk dedicated to President Theodore Roosevelt. The rest of his land would revert to the government at the time of his death. Morrison died in 1932 and is buried in the Conrad Memorial Cemetery in Kalispell.

As Pat and I turned away from Morrison's memorial, the breeze suddenly veered around to the east and picked up sharply. The Canadian cold front had arrived as predicted. Gale-force winds began to squeeze through the mountain passes, booming and shrieking. The tumult was incredible! No wonder some said that the voices of long-dead warriors could be heard on the wind!

Safety and a welcome supper waited for us at the Izaak Walton Inn, just a few miles away, if we could make it. Buffeted by tremendous gusts of wind, we hurried back to our car and, as so many before us had done over the years, fled haunted Marias Pass.

PRINCE OF WALES HOTEL

THE LOW CLOUDS THAT SHROUDED THE MOUNTAINS BEGAN TO lift as we drove steadily toward the Canadian border and Alberta's reputedly haunted Prince of Wales Hotel. To the west, the distinctive outline of 9,000-foot Chief Mountain slowly materialized. Its serrated top bore a strong resemblance to the upright eagle feathers on a Blackfeet war bonnet. Meriwether Lewis, who reportedly viewed the mountain in 1806, called it Tower Mountain, but the Blackfeet name is *Ninaistko*, Mountain Chief.

Chief Mountain is regarded as the home of the Thunderbird by the Blackfeet and is one of many sacred sites in Glacier National Park still used by Native Americans for vision quests. It is said that long ago, a warrior of the enemy Flathead tribe managed to evade the watchful Blackfeet, and held a vision quest on the mountain using a buffalo skull for a pillow. True or not, a partially decomposed buffalo skull was found on Chief Mountain in 1892 by Henry L. Stimson, whose Blackfeet companion reputedly referred to the skull as "the old Flathead's pillow."

The Chief Mountain International Highway is one of the most scenic in the U.S. and is open only in summer. Our journey would take us across the wooded grasslands of the Blackfeet Reservation, through the northeastern tip of Glacier National Park, across the Canadian border at Chief Mountain Port of Entry and eventually to Waterton Lakes National Park.

The mountain gradually receded into the distance as we approached the Port of Entry. The border crossing was uneventful and took only a few minutes. Soon afterward, we spotted a Canadian speed limit sign, posted in kilometers per hour. Oops! I quickly slowed down to the posted 60 kph (37 mph).

For thousands of years, wandering tribes hunted buffalo and other game on the prairie. Traces of their activities have been found at various sites, including Head-Smashed-In Buffalo Jump, about an hour's drive from Waterton. Europeans began to explore the region in the 1800s, and in 1895 Waterton became Canada's fourth national park. In 1911, John George "Kootenai" Brown, a frontiersman who became Waterton's first park superintendent, and Glacier National Park Ranger "Death on the Trail" Reynolds, whose territory included Goat Haunt just across the U.S. border, began to talk about the possibility of linking the two parks. In 1932, their dream came true when far-sighted individuals on both sides of the border helped create the Waterton-Glacier International Peace Park. Waterton also shares with Glacier the rare distinction of being both a World Heritage Site and a Biosphere Reserve.

The townsite of Waterton was established at Upper Waterton Lake in 1910. The town's population drops to about thirty people in the winter, but swells to around two hundred residents during the warmer months. The village also plays host in summer to thousands of tourists from all over the world, who come to enjoy spectacular scenery, boat tours, hiking, scuba diving and wildlife photography. Deer often bed down in people's front yards, seemingly oblivious to cameras clicking away at them.

Although it was only September, a chilly breeze whipped the narrow lake into whitecaps and caused flower baskets to sway as we drove slowly through the town. It was another reminder of how short summers are in the mountains.

Across the bay we could make out the Prince of Wales Hotel on a high bluff overlooking the lake. The distant hotel looked like a child's toy although it is one of the largest wood-framed buildings ever constructed in Alberta. With its steeply pitched roof, gabled windows, balconies and thirty-foot bell tower, the stately seven-storied building is deservedly one of the most photographed buildings in Canada.

The Prince of Wales opened on July 25, 1927, the last of the great railway hotels built by the Great Northern Railway. The remote location made it difficult to transport building materials to the site, and on two occasions, gale force winds shifted the partially-completed building several inches out of position. Heavy cables were installed to anchor the structure securely to the ground. Even with the cables, a gentle swaying motion is sometimes noticeable on the upper floors when strong winds are blowing.

At the hotel's main entrance, a bellman wearing a Royal Stewart kilt greeted us and carried our luggage inside. We followed him into the soaring lobby, with tiered balconies and eighteen-foot-high windows that provide a stunning view of the lake far below. Guests occupied many of the comfortable armchairs, reading or just enjoying the scenery.

The Prince of Wales is open only one hundred days each summer. Although the walls of this historic hotel are thin, the antique elevator only goes up as far as the fourth floor, and faucets sometimes drip during the night, the Prince more than makes up for its few shortcomings with comfortable beds, good food, and sheer baronial splendor.

Registration complete, our luggage disappeared into the elevator with the bellman. We promptly headed for Valerie's Tea Room. It had been a long time since breakfast at Many Glacier and soon we were enjoying delicately-scented tea, pastries, scones, smoked salmon and cucumber sandwiches, chocolate biscuits and enormous fresh strawberries, all served on fine contemporary china. At last the teapot stood empty and only a few crumbs were left on the three-tier server. It was time to meet Chris Barr, the hotel's manager.

"I've heard the ghost stories, but I haven't myself seen anything," Barr told us as we sat in his office overlooking the lobby. "When we're opening up the hotel in the spring, all the windows have boards and sheets are still over the furniture. Walking into the hotel by yourself with all the creaking is definitely eerie. The building still gives me the jitters because of the wind.

"This year, we had some of our housekeepers working on the sixth floor of the hotel, and all of a sudden I heard this screaming coming down the hallway and I thought, 'What's going on?'

"They said 'Chris, when we were cleaning that room, all the water was off. We stepped out for two minutes and when we went back in all the water was turned on.'

"There's also supposed to be a ghost wearing a stovepipe hat in the basement," Barr continued. "An employee who saw him said he looks like Abraham Lincoln."

Barr then handed us a black-and-white photograph of the lobby. "We had a couple of newspaper reporters in the hotel about ten or fifteen years ago," he said. "They wanted a photo of the lobby when it was empty, so one of them decided to come down about 2 o'clock in the morning. When he developed the photo, this is what he got."

The photo had been taken sometime after 1958, when the original rustic furniture was replaced with a more traditional style. Several semi-transparent figures of men wearing old-fashioned suits are visible in the foreground. Others can be seen on the balconies of the lobby. Their features are unclear, and their legs are blurred below the knees.

Thanks to modern photo-editing software, thousands of "ghost" photographs are circulating on the internet. Most can be debunked as fakes. Pat, an accomplished photographer, suggested that we try to duplicate the photo late that evening. Perhaps we could determine whether it was a double exposure.

"Some people don't want anything to do with a haunting," Barr observed. "We don't go out of our way to broadcast it. And there are some who will come specifically because of the ghost stories."

We'd been assigned a room on the second floor, but Barr generously offered us room 510 instead. This was one of the rooms said to be haunted by "Sarah" or "Sara," a former employee who fell in love with the manager many years ago. He did not return her affections, and she threw herself to her death from a window. Guests had reportedly sensed a presence in that room and occasionally a window left open overnight would be found closed in the morning.

We thanked Mr. Barr warmly and left with a promise to let him know if anything unusual happened during the night. The elevator arrived shortly to take us to the fourth floor, where a stairway led up to our new room on the fifth floor.

The bellman operating the elevator was a young man with a French accent. He had heard stories about the hotel, but dismissed most of them as legend. In the lobby, however, something had occurred that puzzled him. "Different times you will hear someone walking toward you," he said. "They are heavy footsteps, like a man, you know? But no one is there."

Room 510 was larger than we'd expected, with a queen-sized bed and dark wainscoting typical of the era in which the hotel was built. Windows overlooked a narrow balcony. The room had no television or internet service, but the view of the mountains and lake more than made up for it.

Pat and I had brought some ghost hunting equipment with us, so we quickly did a sweep of the room with an EMF (electromagnetic field) meter. The readings were normal. Next, we asked questions aloud, using our digital recorders. If "Sarah" or other spirits were present in the room, we hoped to capture a disembodied reply. On playback, however, we heard nothing but our own voices. Undaunted, we set a child's toy and one of Pat's earrings on the bed, noted their exact positions, and left the room. Perhaps something would move one of the objects while we were gone.

Chris Barr had suggested that we interview the staff, so we began with the bellmen. One of the stories they told us involved a chef who supposedly murdered his wife back in the days when employees were housed on the sixth floor. The chef's wife had been having an affair, and when he discovered it, he stabbed her and hid her body in a closet. He then fled the hotel and was never seen again.

Guests in Room 608, where the murder is thought to have occurred, have occasionally felt someone tuck them in at night. A humorous account of one such encounter was posted by David Ellis on the Australian travel site webwombat.com. According to Ellis, an American tourist who'd "shared a whiskey or ten with his fellow anglers" was awakened during the night by someone tucking him in. He turned on the lights but saw no one. It happened once more, and again the still somewhat boozy angler turned on the lights. No one was there. Perplexed and a little uneasy, he left the lights on the rest of the night. When he told his friends about it at breakfast the next morning, they laughed it off—until their waiter, who had overheard the story, told them about the ghost.

Bellman Will Johnston doesn't put much stock in those stories, but he did have an odd experience when he tried to open the door to 608 during his first season at the hotel.

"I went to open the door, put the key into it, and none of the keys would actually go into the slot. Then I put the skeleton key in and it wouldn't work. It was really, really weird. Then I tried a different key that's actually designed for 608 because it's a different lock, and it wouldn't work."

He's not the only one who has had trouble with keys. Former manager Gayle Jensen told the *Lethbridge Herald* on May 31, 2000, about a time when chambermaids needed to get into a room, but the door wouldn't open. "Finally, I said 'Sarah, I need to get into this room, cut it out.' The door opened. Another time we had a door locked but the chain was on, and the chain can't be put on if nobody's in the room. No one was in the room."

The murderous chef wasn't the only ghost, according to employees. They told us several versions of "Sarah's" story. In some versions, Sarah jumped to her death from Room 510, where we would be staying that night; in other versions, it was 516. According to Red Bus driver Robert Lucke, Room 516 was the scene of a strange occurrence when another driver spent a night there with his wife. The driver claimed that a female ghost got into bed with him while his wife slept peacefully by his side!

Later that afternoon we drove down to the marina for our long-anticipated excursion aboard the motor vessel *International*. The boat has provided entertaining tours of Waterton Lake since 1927 and crosses the international boundary, marked by clear-cuts through the forest on both sides of the lake, on the way to Goat Haunt, a U.S. port-of-entry in neighboring Glacier National Park. Open only during the summer, Goat Haunt is accessible by boat or on foot. We docked for half an hour at Goat Haunt to visit the International Peace Park Pavilion. Several hikers returning from the back country joined us for the voyage back to Waterton. Although the deep, fjord-like lake was choppy, the ride was smooth and we enjoyed watching for bear, deer, moose and eagles along the shore.

Pat and I savored an excellent late supper of Welsh rarebit in the Royal Stewart Dining Room. By the time we finished our ice cream, it was almost closing time. Suddenly we both caught a strong whiff of cigarette smoke. The hotel has a no-smoking policy and we instinctively looked around for the culprit. None of the few guests left in the restaurant was smoking and the windows were not open. Since no one else seemed to be aware of it, we just shrugged it off and left.

Back in the nearly-deserted lobby, Pat took photos from different angles and with different exposures, hoping to duplicate the photograph Chris Barr had shown us. At 10:30 P.M. a bellman announced the last elevator run of the evening. Rather than climb five flights of stairs with a bad knee, Pat got aboard. I made myself comfortable in an armchair near the darkened windows that now reflected the interior of the lobby.

The hotel gradually settled down for the night. The wind had died, as mountain winds often do after sunset. There would be no chance to experience the hotel's notorious sway that night. As I gazed around the baronial lobby, I thought of those who had visited the hotel long ago. Did they sometimes gather in the quiet hours of the night to relive happy memories of long-ago days? I couldn't fault them if they did.

Eventually the night auditors came on duty, and I introduced myself to Tasha and a co-worker. Tasha had worked two seasons at the hotel. She was aware of the ghost stories and had noticed a few odd things herself.

"There's supposed to be a ghost in the Royal Stewart Dining Room," she told me. "He smokes there in the middle of the night. Sometimes I've gone in there on break and I can actually smell cigarette smoke."

Her coworker had been hovering nearby, listening. "I've smelled it too," she put in. "Sometimes I walk through the restaurant around 2 A.M. when I go to get my food on break and I'll smell the smoke. There's never anyone around, and the windows are closed. "

My ears pricked up at that. "That's odd," I told them, "because my friend and I just had dinner in there tonight and we both smelled fresh cigarette smoke quite near us. We thought maybe the man at the next table was a smoker and that smoke might be clinging to his clothes. We walked right past him on the way out, though, and the odor wasn't coming from him."

Tasha nodded. "Yeah, that's probably the most common one. There's another one in the basement, a man who wears a tall hat and leaves the smell of pipe smoke behind."

"Anything else you can't explain?" I asked.

"Well, the emergency exit flew open by itself one night," Tasha's coworker said, "and it wasn't windy out. There are weird creaky noises even when the wind isn't blowing. And we'll hear footsteps on the balconies. We'll think it must be guests and go look. No one is there."

It's possible, of course, that guests may have briefly stepped out of their rooms. That doesn't explain the disembodied footsteps that approached the French-speaking bellman in the empty lobby, nor does it explain the footsteps heard by a former staff member running down the stairs from the sixth floor when the hotel was closed and boarded up for the winter.

Tasha added, "One time I was checking in guests who had one of the haunted rooms, 510 or 608, about 4 A.M. The elevator doesn't run all night, so I had to carry their luggage up for them. The lights are off at night and all the doors are shut, but when I got up there, all the lights were on and all the doors open. Another time, the housekeepers changed all the glasses in 608, and when they came back to inspect the room, one of the glasses was full of water. No one else had been into the room."

By now it was nearly one A.M. The elevator had shut down at 10:30 P.M. so I thanked the two night auditors and began the long trek up five flights of stairs. The hotel was eerily silent as I padded along the corridor to Room 510. Pat opened the door at my knock, clearly relieved to see me. She'd heard footsteps in the corridor twice during the evening. Once they'd paused just outside our door. There'd been no knock and no sound of retreating footsteps. Cautiously, she'd opened the door. No one was there, nor was anyone visible along the corridor.

Nothing disturbed us during the night, however, and I awoke

early. Two large bucks sparred in a meadow that bordered the lake. Below, a doe and her fawn grazed peacefully on the grass just outside the hotel's entrance. Pat and I watched, enthralled, until the two deer ambled off in the direction of the town.

After a late breakfast, it was time to leave the Prince of Wales. While we were packing, we both heard a rat-tat-tat on our door, as if someone had rapped on the wooden panels with his knuckles. Pat was standing next to the door and opened it on the third knock, expecting to see a housekeeper standing there. No one was there, although a housekeeping cart stood in front of a room far down the hall. It didn't seem humanly possible for someone to have tapped on our door and run all the way to the other room before Pat looked out. But then, maybe whoever tapped *wasn't* human.

When we reached the border crossing, the traffic was held up for a few minutes by a group of visiting dignitaries who were surrounded by news crews. To our delight, a group of Royal Canadian Mounted Police in traditional boots and red jackets formed an honor guard at the side of the road. We'd both grown up in the 1950s watching broadcasts of *Sergeant Preston of the Yukon* with its thrilling theme music, the *Donna Diana Overture*, and decided to pretend that the Mounties were there to escort us to the border. As we drove past, we waved, and I *think* one of them gave us a wink in return.

Is the Prince of Wales haunted? If not, it probably should be, for it has all the elements of a good ghost story: a romantic old hotel, a reputed murder, and a suicide. Throw in its isolated location, the unnerving wind, and Hollywood could hardly find a better setting.

Unfortunately for legend, there is no historical evidence that a murder ever took place at the hotel. Truth is seldom allowed to get in the way of a good story, however, so the legend of the homicidal chef persists despite attempts by historians to debunk it. A suicide did occur at the hotel. According to a brief article in the *Lethbridge Herald*, Aug. 2, 1977, a twenty-year-old woman, a seasonal employee from Quebec, jumped naked from a sixth story window of the Prince of Wales Hotel. Her body was discovered about 5:30 P.M. on the flagstones on the south side of the hotel.

Contrary to popular opinion, a suicide does not inevitably cause a haunting. If "Sarah" (not the woman's actual name) is not responsible for the odd experiences reported by staff and guests, are there other explanations? I asked Ray Djuff, who wrote *High on a Windy Hill*, the meticulously-researched history of the Prince of Wales, for his opinion. Djuff, who worked at the hotel in the 1970s, is skeptical of most of the claims.

"The young lady upon whom I believe the "Sarah" legend was based did not live in the hotel," he said. "She lived in the dorms, so rooms 510 or 516 could not have been where she stayed."

He believes that the cigarette smoke in the dining room can be explained by employees who take a cigarette break near the trash from the staff cafeteria. "On those occasions when the wind is coming from the north or west, the cigarette smoke will get blown to the front of the hotel, where there are fans in the dining room that can draw in the smoke."

The wind was from the south the day Pat and I smelled the cigarette smoke, though, and in any case I'm not convinced that the smoke would be localized around a particular table, but Djuff's explanation certainly is possible. As far as the emergency exit flying open by itself, he said, "If an outside fire exit door is not fully closed at the end of the hallway, and someone opens one of the hallway fire doors at the lobby end of the hallway, there can be enough difference in air pressure that it will cause the emergency exit to open, possibly even to 'fly open by itself.'"

What does he think about the footsteps reported by so many employees, footsteps that my friend Pat heard come up to our door and stop, or the raps on our door as we prepared to leave?

"I like to think I can explain it all," he continued, "but I know I can't. Are the footsteps attributable to some paranormal thing? No idea for sure. I know it doesn't take much to get creeped out, though."

Pat and I certainly were "creeped out" when we played back the taped interview with hotel manager Chris Barr. I always use fresh, high-quality audiotape for an interview and never tape on both sides, yet an unfamiliar female voice broke in during the interview. Her words cannot be made out, even with audio software. Only Chris Barr, Pat, and I were in the office room at the time.

It seems that the Prince of Wales may have at least one "permanent guest" after all.

SPOOKY SPERRY

On a cool September morning more than thirty years ago I set out in search of adventure. My goal was to hike the notoriously difficult 6.7-mile hike from Lake McDonald lodge to Sperry Chalet. There are only two ways to reach this historic backcountry chalet: on foot or by saddle horse. As the saying goes, it all depends on where you like your blisters!

I'd read that the trail was grueling, rugged, not for casual hikers. Although I was an experienced hiker, up to this point my hiking had been limited to flatland trails. For a moment I wavered; could I really handle a mountain trail that gained over 3500 feet in altitude? There was only one way to find out. I took a deep breath and laced up my boots.

The trail began across the road from the Lake McDonald parking lot. Several riders were settling into their saddles as I approached, and I followed them into an old growth forest of cedar and hemlock. As the trail began to rise, the trees were replaced by pine and fir, better adapted to higher terrain. More than once I had to edge off the trail to allow a rider or a downward-bound string of pack mules to pass by. Some of the hikers behind me had already turned back.

By the time I'd reached the footbridge over Snyder Creek about two miles from the trailhead, my leg muscles were burning. A little farther on, they started to cramp. I sat down on a large rock and massaged my sore feet and rubbery legs while I considered my options. I knew that from this point on the trail steepened, with switchbacks, boulders and loose shale. The altitude was beginning to affect me too, making it harder to catch my breath.

Although I was tempted to turn around, I continued to follow the group on horseback, now far above me. It was probably not a good decision. A tired hiker may become careless, and in Glacier, a misstep can be deadly. Over the years there have been more than two hundred fifty deaths in the park, many of them caused by falls.

Eventually, the thin air at higher elevations proved too much for me. I had to turn back before I reached the chalet. I wasn't disappointed though; I'd exceeded my expectations and had an unforgettable adventure!

Glacier's great lodges and backcountry chalets are inextricably linked with James J. Hill, president of the Great Northern Railway. As early as 1891, Hill saw the profit potential in a link between his railroad and the new national park proposed by conservationist George Bird Grinnell. When legislation to create the park later stalled in Congress, Grinnell asked the influential Hill for help.

The railroad baron spoke, and Congress listened. On May 11, 1910, the nation's tenth national park was finally established. Barely a month later work began on the network of chalets and hotels that Hill and his son Louis hoped would lure rail passengers to the pristine wilderness the Hills proclaimed "the American Alps."

Of the nine backcountry chalets built by railroad construction crews between 1910 and 1915, only Sperry Chalet and Granite Park Chalet remain. Constructed primarily of native stone by Italian stonemasons, Sperry and Granite Park have survived almost a century of harsh alpine winters, although Sperry had a close call in early 2011 when an avalanche caused considerable damage. Cut Bank, St. Mary, Going-to-the-Sun, Many Glacier, Goat Haunt and Gunsight Lake chalets are long gone, their wooden structures destroyed by forest fires, avalanches, or the ravages of time. Only the kitchen/dining hall building, now a camp store, remains of the Two Medicine Chalet.

Sperry Chalet sits on a rocky ledge with a magnificent view of waterfalls, jagged peaks, and, far below, Lake McDonald. Begun in 1913, the chalet complex opened the following year. The original two-story dormitory with its wooden porches and the single-story kitchen/dining room are still in use, little changed over the years, but the pit toilets have been replaced by a new composting restroom building with sinks.

In 1987 the chalet became a National Historic Landmark. The letters *G N Ry* picked out in stone at one end of the dormitory are a lasting reminder of the Great Northern Railway's importance in the history of Glacier National Park.

Many of Sperry's guests are seasoned outdoorsmen and women who make Sperry their base for a few days. Others are campers or day trippers who drop in for lunch or a slice of the chalet's famous berry pie. Hiking is a popular activity, with the 3.5-mile trek to Comeau Pass and Sperry Glacier a favorite. Both the glacier and the chalet were named for Dr. Lyman B. Sperry, who had been asked by the railroad to look for scenic attractions that might interest its passengers. Sperry was among the first to reach the glacier in 1896. Other trails lead to Lincoln Peak, Gunsight Pass and Lake Ellen Wilson. Mountain goats are frequently encountered by hikers along the trails, and grizzlies have occasionally been seen.

Accommodations at Sperry Chalet are rustic but comfortable. Meals, bed linens, blankets and towels are provided. Overnight guests are advised that they need bring only "a toothbrush and a smile." The dining room has propane lights and a wood stove that provides cozy warmth on chilly days, but the dorm's seventeen guest rooms have no lights, heat, or water. Candles and fueled lights are not permitted, so flashlights are used at night.

It must be eerie, lying awake in the darkness, listening to un-familiar noises just beyond the windows. Guests during the summer of 1931 certainly thought so; many of them were spooked by bearded white faces that stared into the windows at night.

"It was at first thought that Sperry was infested with ghosts," stated the *Helena Daily Independent* on November 1, 1931, "but a Sperry Glacier guide later admitted that he had baited the area around the chalet with salt to attract mountain goats at night. As many as twenty-seven goats were counted one night. These 'ghosts' were easily routed, however. One night someone put pepper on the windowsills instead of salt and the entire herd departed amid sounds of great sneezing."

Curious to find out whether there had been any more recent reports of spooks at Sperry, I contacted General Manager Kevin Warrington. He assured me that since his family took over operations at Sperry and Granite Park chalets three generations ago, there has not been a single ghost story.

I like to imagine that everyone who visits this beautiful park leaves a trace of themselves behind. Perhaps Seasonal Ranger Doug Follett, who recently completed fifty years with the National Park Service, said it best in the conclusion of his poem "The Spirits of Sperry":

> *And as you leave*
> *When it's time to go*
> *And you stop to wave*
> *From the trail below*
> *I think you'll see*
> *With the Sperry crew*
> *Your spirit—*
> *Waving back at you.*

(With thanks to Doug Follett)

TWO MEDICINE VALLEY

WE'D BEEN WARNED TO EXPECT CONSTRUCTION DELAYS ON Montana Route 49, a Going-to-the-Sun wannabe with frost-heaved pavement, switchbacks, missing guardrails and trucks that hurtle around blind corners. But Route 49 had even more to offer us: a herd of Angus cattle, placidly gazing at us from the middle of the narrow road. I braked, coming to a gentle stop almost nose-to-nose with a half-ton steer. He snorted but stood his ground. This was, after all, open range, and cattle had right-of-way.

Pat and I exchanged glances, thinking of the badly-shaken driver we'd met at our motel in St. Mary the previous night. Still a bit wild-eyed, he'd told us that he'd left East Glacier en route to St. Mary at twilight. Just past Looking Glass Hill a black mass suddenly loomed up in front of him. He'd had to swerve violently to avoid a huge black cow bedded down on the warm pavement.

I eased ahead very slowly, and the herd parted just as slowly before us. Our destination was the Two Medicine Valley, some-times called Glacier's "secret" valley, long considered to be sacred by the Blackfeet and other Native American tribes. But Route 49 has a secret of its own: it parallels an amazing network of pre-historic trails called the Old North Trail. The 10,000-year-old trails ran from northern Canada all the way to Mexico and were used for trade, warfare, and visiting distant relatives. According to Mathilde Holtz, author of *Glacier National Park: Its Trails and Treasures* (1917), the trail was marked by piles of whitened bones, both human and animal, well into the 20th century.

Ethnologist and historian Walter McClintock spent three years with the Blackfeet and later wrote *The Old North Trail, or, Life, Legends and Religion of the Blackfeet*. He traveled parts of the trail with the Blackfeet several times and jotted down the great spiritual leader Brings-down-the-Sun's account of the trail:

> There is a well known trail we call the Old North Trail. It runs north and south along the Rocky Mountains. No one knows how long it has been used by the Indians. My father told me it originated in the migration of a great tribe of Indians from the distant north to the south, and all the tribes have, ever since, continued to follow in their tracks. The Old North Trail is now becoming overgrown with moss and grass, but it was worn so deeply, by many generations of travelers, that the travois tracks and horse trail are still plainly visible.
>
> On Crow Lodge River, just across from our present camp, a lone pine tree once stood. It was a land-mark for people travelling north and south along the Old North Trail, because it stood upon the plain and could be seen from a long distance. Finally the Lone Tree fell, but two children took its place. They have grown large and now they mark the former course of the North Trail. The Indians still speak of the spot as the Lone Tree. In many places the white man's roads and towns have obliterated the Old Trail. It forked where the city of Calgary now stands. The right fork ran north into the Barren Lands as far as people live. The main trail ran south along the eastern side of the Rockies, at a uniform distance from the mountains, keeping clear of the forest, and outside of the foothills. It ran close to where the city of Helena now stands, and extended south into the country, inhabited by a people with dark skins, and long hair falling

over their faces (Mexico).

In former times, when the Indian tribes were at war, there was constant fighting along the North Trail. In those days, Indians, who wanted to travel in peace, avoided it and took to the forest. My father once told me of an expedition from the Blackfeet, that went south by the Old Trail, to visit the people with dark skins. Elk Tongue and his wife, Natoya, were of this expedition, also Arrow Top and Pemmican, who was a boy of twelve at that time. He died only a few years ago at the age of ninety-five. They were absent four years. It took them twelve moons of steady travelling to reach the country of the dark skinned people, and eighteen moons to come north again."

The Old North Trail was used by the Blackfeet as recently as the 1930s to visit relatives in Canada, but disuse has allowed grass to gradually obscure the ruts worn by the travois poles dragged by dogs and, much later, horses. Faint traces of those ruts are said to be still visible on Two Medicine Ridge, to the north of Route 49. Circles of stones which once held down the edges of tipi covers can also be found along the trail, and rock cairns that may have been prehistoric trail markers.

For a moment I pictured myself sitting quietly beside one of those stone cairns atop Two Medicine Ridge on a warm summer day, knowing that for thousands of years, uncounted numbers of people had walked that same trail. Why had they set out on a journey of thousands of miles? Whose hand built the cairns, and what was their purpose? Do the Old Ones ever return in spirit to walk the trails again?

Someday, I promised myself, I would walk in their footsteps, at least for a little while.

As we approached the Two Medicine turnoff, the sun broke through thinning clouds, and we caught glimpses of Lower Two

Medicine Lake sparkling between the trees.

The excursion boat *Sinopah* was pulling away from the dock for a tour of the lake as we parked nearby. On the far side of the lake rose Mount Sinopah, named for Hugh Monroe's Blackfeet wife, its pyramidal peak silhouetted by the late afternoon sun.

The Two Medicine Valley is quiet now, overlooked by most even at the height of the summer season, but it hasn't always been that way. In the days before automobiles were common, visitors arrived at East Glacier or Belton by train. They toured the park on horseback, staying at the Great Northern Railway's hotels or rustic chalets, each spaced a day's ride apart. Of the backcountry chalets, only Sperry and Granite Park still remain.

The valley has historic associations with President Franklin Delano Roosevelt, who broadcast one of his signature "fireside chats" from the Two Medicine Chalet in 1934. The chalet was razed in 1956, but the massive log building that once housed the dining hall and kitchen survives today as a busy camp store.

The area is also of great historical importance to the four bands of the Blackfoot Nation: the Kainai, or Bloods, the Piikani, or Northern Piegans, the Siksika, or Blackfoot, all located in Alberta, and the Southern Piegans, or Blackfeet, based in Montana. As Darrell Norman, historian, artist and member of the Blackfeet tribe, explained, "Our territory ran to north of Calgary, south to the Yellowstone River, west to the Rocky Mountain and east three-fourths of the way across Montana. In the summertime we'd come up here to gather wood and berries and medicine and hunt in the fall, but by wintertime we would move away.

"There are still deserted camps with circles where teepees had stood. Smallpox would kill entire camps, and spirits would hang around for a while. We wrapped people in buffalo robes with their belongings and put them up on scaffolds on the side of cliffs or natural places. When on the move, we would cover them with rocks, not bury them. For a period of time, even up to the 1920s, they would build ghost houses. People would avoid those places, because they would see swirly blue lights."

As far back as the 1890s there were reports of ghosts seen near the scaffold burials in the valley. One of those encounters was recorded by Walter McClintock in *The Old North Trail*.

Strikes-on-both-Sides said, "There have been many ghosts this summer bothering people who travel near the Two Medicine River at night. Old Person was recently riding down the river to Little Plume's. When he was passing the cottonwood trees, where the dead bodies lie in the branches, his horse suddenly reared and plunged, as if frightened by an apparition. Then Old Person heard a voice speaking from the trees, saying, 'Old Person! What has delayed your coming to the spirit world so long? I have been waiting for you a very long time.' He was so badly frightened he rode away at a gallop. Next day he was taken sick and in a few days he died. I also heard of another case. When Big Wolf Medicine and Buffalo Hide were recently camped on the Two Medicine with their wives, a ghost harassed them all night, so that they could not sleep.

The Blackfeet believe that spirits, or *staah*, are around them on a daily basis. "They make whistling sounds," Darrell Norman told us, "and try to get you to go with them to the Sand Hills. The Sand Hills is an area south of the Saskatchewan River where you go when you die. The place is very much like where you're living today, only in a spirit world. We cannot see the spirits, but we can feel their presence."

Spirit energies can linger for a long time, according to Norman. There are powerful energies in the Two Medicine Valley also, especially around Running Eagle Falls and the buffalo jumps, where for centuries Native Americans stampeded bison over cliffs to obtain their winter's supply of meat.

Although the spirits may seem menacing at times, they can also be helpful. George Kicking Horse told Norman about a man who was working near Heart Butte, about twenty-five miles from home.

It was November, and a storm blew up. The man started back home on his horse, but the storm turned into a blizzard with winds of seventy miles per hour. He saw a light on the prairie and headed toward it. When he got close, he saw it was a small ranch house with a barn. He tied up his horse and went inside the house. A man was there, and he said, "Put your horse in the barn and you can stay here and have something to eat."

He did as the man told him, and after he had eaten he sat by the fire for a while to warm himself. Then the man said, "You can sleep upstairs." He went up to bed. When he woke up, the warm quilts were gone and he was lying on the bare coil springs of the bed. He walked downstairs. The whole cabin was dilapidated and no one was there. When he went out to the barn his horse was there but there was no hay. He'd encountered a friendly ghost who'd helped him through the night.

According to Norman, there are many areas of spiritual significance in Glacier and Waterton Lakes national parks. To the Blackfeet, the most sacred site is Chief Mountain on the northeast corner of Glacier Park. "People go there to pray and go on vision quests," he said. "It's the home of the Thunderbird. Getting as high and close to the sun as possible is very important."

A Blackfeet legend links Chief Mountain to the Two Medicine Valley.

Many years ago there was a famine in the land of the

Blackfeet. At that time the Blackfeet Indians owned everything from Hudson Bay to the Rocky Mountains, and in all that land there was no green spot except in the valley that is called Two Medicine. Even the buffalo left the country because there was no food for them and the Indians that sought refuge in the mountains found no game or anything to eat except berries.

Then the old men of the tribe withdrew to the valley that is now called Two Medicine and built there two medicine lodges, so great was their need. They worshipped the Great Spirit and prayed to be told what they should do to be saved from the famine. And the Great Spirit heard them and directed them to send seven of their patriarchs to the Chief Mountain, where the wind god was then residing.

They followed those directions and seven of their oldest men retired to Chief Mountain, and there surely was the wind god. He stood at the summit of the mountain and the wings extending from his shoulders spread wide over the valleys. He faced north, east, south and west and his wings quivered as he stood. The old men worshipped him from afar, but were afraid to come near him to make their prayers, and after their long journey they went back empty handed to their people.

Then the medicine men directed them to send eleven of their strongest and bravest young warriors to intercede with the wind god. These young men also, when they reached the mountain and saw the wind god, were afraid, but they drew nearer and nearer to him and finally they dared to touch the skins he was wearing. They made their prayer to him and he listened. His wings quivered and quivered and gradually clouds began to gather over the plains and the rain fell as if in a deluge. He stretched one wing wide over the plain, telling them to go back there and they would find the buffalo. [*Anaconda Standard*, February 8, 1914].

The Two Medicine Valley is said to have gotten its name when two of the tribes of the Blackfeet Confederacy held an *Okan*, or Sun Dance, at the same time on opposite banks of a river. From then on, the area was called Two Medicine Lodges. The valley is still an important spiritual center where Blackfeet still go to pray and leave medicine bundles.

One of the most sacred sites is Running Eagle Falls, named for a renowned woman warrior who lived in the early nineteenth century. Given the name Weasel Woman as a child, the girl had little interest in domestic chores. She was taught to use a bow by her father and became an expert horsewoman and hunter. One day their hunting party was attacked by enemies and her father was killed. The girl put her father's body and the buffalo meat on her horse and escaped. It was the first of many adventures that would earn her a respected place in Blackfeet history.

When she was twenty, Weasel Woman was allowed to join a war party on a horse-stealing raid. She stole six fine horses from the Flatheads. On her return home, she was given the name Pitamakan, or Running Eagle, the only Piegan woman ever to earn a man's name. She was also the only woman to undertake a grueling vision quest. The place chosen for such a quest must be remote and perilous, on mountain peaks or narrow ledges, and those attempting the quest must be able to endure four days without food or water. Running Eagle is said to have slept in a cave above a waterfall, where she received her vision and her power.

At thirty, she went on a raid against the Flathead Indians and was clubbed down from behind. Her Piegan warriors brought her back to Upper Two Medicine Lake and buried her in a tree on the mountain overlooking the falls.

Intrigued by the story of Running Eagle, Pat and I decided to hike to the waterfall named for her. The falls was once known as Trick Falls, because it consists of an upper and lower falls. During spring runoff, the flow from the upper falls obscures the lower falls. It was an easy stroll through trees and shrubs already showing hints of autumnal color, and we arrived at the falls to find that we were the only ones there. This late in the season, the upper falls were dry and the stream spilled into a shallow plunge pool from the lower falls.

A haze of smoke from a distant forest fire partially obscured the lowering sun, which cast an eerie reddish light on the scene. The only sounds were the splashing of the lower falls and the occasional click as Pat's boots struck a rock. As we approached the falls the atmosphere seemed to change subtly and Pat, who is part Cherokee, told me that she felt a deep sense of spirituality there, as if it were a holy place. The hair at the back of my neck bristled; at that moment I could certainly believe we were in the presence of powerful energies. We took several photos, and then stood quietly for a few minutes, paying silent respect to a great Blackfeet warrior who will forever be held in high esteem and honor by her people.

On our way back to Saint Mary, I had to resist a strong urge to stop and explore Two Medicine Ridge and its prehistoric pathway. Unfortunately, I hadn't brought hiking boots along nor did we have the time to climb up to the Old North Trail with its tipi rings and stone cairns.

When I happened to mention my interest in the trail to Seasonal Ranger Doug Follett later, he told me, "Those stones are symbols of all the history that has taken place there." Then he shared a poem he'd written that powerfully evokes those long-ago days.

Tipi Rings

So I stood alone not long ago
on the great high plains where the north winds blow.
The real stones circle round

Like a necklace there upon the ground,
A necklace placed by some small hand
To hold the lodge skins to the land
And to the poles that stretched so high
Like fingers holding up the sky.
And I wondered what those stones had seen,
And what their stories might have been.
Did buffalo in an endless sea
Pass by this place like you and me?
Did painted men on painted steeds
Count coup here in glorious deeds?
And what of those with eyes so pale?
Did they walk here, on the Beaver Trail?
The sacred peaks rise there to the west.
Did the trail start here, for a vision quest?
Did children play in the prairie grass
And chase the tumbleweeds as they passed?
To hear them sing as they raced along,
"We're wild! We're free!" And now they're gone.
And now they're gone.
And what I found is all that's left here on the ground:
A circle of stone welcomes you and me
to the tipi rings so silently.

(With warm thanks to Doug Follett)

THE CAVE AT BELLY RIVER

Who doesn't love old-fashioned campfire stories, the creepier the better? This one is set along the Belly River, a remote and unspoiled area of lodgepole pine and aspen forest ideal for hikers who enjoy solitude. Jerry Black relates the story passed down to him by his grandfather, former park ranger Hugh Black:

THERE'S A HIKER WHO WANTS TO GET OFF THE TRAIL AWAY FROM where people are and he's working his way up this old creek bed when he comes across a little chasm in the rocks. There aren't many caves in Glacier so he wants to go explore it. So he goes in and he's got a flashlight so he's working his way along with his flashlight and the cave opens up a bit. He finds it's a pretty extensive system, but he starts getting a little prickle on the back of his neck. He figures it's just from being in a cave, but he shines the flashlight around and sees nothing. He winds his way through tight passages, and the cave opens up again, then he has to crawl through more passages. If you're claustrophobic it's not a good feeling. His flashlight starts to fade but he thinks, "OK, I've got lots of matches and it's a straightforward deal to get out because I didn't see any forks," so he goes on a little farther and the cave seems to be opening up. He thinks he sees a little light ahead, but he's not sure he really sees it.

Just then his flashlight goes out. Immediately he gets more

prickles on the back of his neck. "Okay, stay calm," he says to himself, rummaging around in his pack for matches. The faint light seems stronger, so he decides to work toward it, feeling his way along and lighting matches now and then. After a while he starts lighting more and more matches because he feels something nearby. He thinks he sees something scoot off, all bent over, but he's not sure of it. Now the dim light seems stronger, so he fumbles his way toward it.

He's getting quite close to it, and he sees the light is coming through a crack in the wall maybe twenty feet up. It definitely leads to the outside, because he can see the light of day out there. But he also sees the skeleton of an old trapper wearing a few shreds of clothes. Then he notices another skeleton in a corner. This one has no remnants of clothes, and a bunch of other bones and small things scattered around. He's trying to figure how he can get out of the cave. The crack isn't very big and he'd have to climb up the wall to reach it. He doesn't know if he'll fit through. All the time he's feeling that prickle at the back of his neck. He lights another match and looks behind him again into the darkness. He seems to see something skinny and all hunched over duck back out of sight. He knows it's after him at this point. He tosses his old Army canteen with his initials scratched into it out the crack in the wall and lights his last match. It goes out.

Weeks later, the canteen is found in the little creek bed. He is never seen again.

POSTSCRIPT

Wherever we wander in magnificent Glacier National Park and beautiful Waterton Lakes National Park, we follow in the footsteps of those who came before us: Native Americans, trappers, hunters, explorers and others whose spirits even today may roam the land they loved so much in life. As Chief Seattle allegedly said,

Our dead never forget this beautiful world that gave them being. They still love its verdant valleys, its murmuring rivers, its magnificent mountains, sequestered vales and verdant lined lakes and bays, and ever yearn in tender fond affection over the lonely hearted living, and often return from the happy hunting ground to visit, guide, console, and comfort them.

Do you have a question or comment about Glacier's ghosts? Would you like to share an eerie experience? You can reach me by email at kstevensp@cs.com. I enjoy hearing from readers! Although I travel much of the year, I will respond as quickly as possible. And check out my website at www.hauntedmontana.com for monthly updates on the most haunted places in Montana.

See you in Glacier!

ABOUT THE AUTHOR

In Karen Stevens own words:

"My fascination with ghosts began at an early age. When I was seven, my parents bought a brick and stucco house in Minneapolis. The house had been built in 1920 and had an air of quiet distinction about it. It didn't take us long, however, to find out that we shared our house with something or someone we couldn't see. At first, it was just a sense of an unseen presence. My father had fixed up a playroom in the basement for us, but my sister and I never liked to play down there. After a few minutes we would become aware that someone was standing in the doorway glaring at us. Although we never saw anyone, we sensed that it was male and that he didn't like little kids. The feeling of dislike would quickly become so intense that we would run upstairs to find our mother.

"A few months later, we began to hear footsteps coming up the stairs from the basement. No one was ever there when we opened the door to look down the stairs. My father was a rational man, trained as a chemist, and he didn't believe us when my sister and I told him that the house was haunted. Something happened one evening, though, that made even my father have second thoughts. We were having supper at the kitchen table. The door to the basement was closed as usual. Suddenly the doorknob began to turn back and forth as if someone were standing on the other side of the door. My father got quietly to his feet and yanked the door open. Nothing was there—nothing that we could see, that is. He was never able to explain that incident to his satisfaction—or ours.

"An unanswered question has always been, to me, an irresistible challenge. Perhaps that's why I find paranormal investigation so fascinating. There are no easy answers, only more questions. How could something without a physical body manage to flick on the dining room light? Why did we all hear footsteps coming up the stairs from the basement when no one was there? Who rang the doorbell but left no tracks in the fresh snow? My father must have grown tired of the barrage of questions, but he never discouraged me from looking for answers.

"Seeking information, I devoured every book the local library had on ghosts. None had the answers I wanted, so I decided to experiment. Unfortunately, it never occurred to me to ask Mom's permission first. She wasn't at all pleased about the flour I sprinkled on the basement floor (no, the ghost didn't leave footprints) and made me clean it up. Then I had an even better idea: to see whether the ghost could pass through a strand of yarn that I'd tacked across the basement stairs. Dad tripped over the yarn, however, and my "junior scientist" experiments came to an abrupt end!

"Over the past half century I've spent many enjoyable days and nights roaming haunted castles, plantation houses and abandoned prisons in search of ghosts. Often we'd go home with nothing to show for a night's vigil but stiff necks and sore feet, but looking back, I wouldn't have missed a moment of it!

"May you too, enjoy many ghostly adventures!"

Karen Stevens is also the author of *Haunted Montana* and *More Hunted Montana*. She lives in Billings, Montana.

SPOOKY TALES AND MORE!

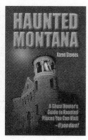

Yellowstone Ghost Stories
by Shellie Larios

Grand Canyon Ghost Stories
by Debe Branning

Glacier Ghost Stories
by Karen Stevens

Haunted Montana
by Karen Stevens

More Haunted Montana
by Karen Stevens

Montana Ghost Stories
by Debra D. Munn

Wyoming Ghost Stories
by Debra D. Munn

Montana UFOs
by Joan Bird

Available from your local bookstore or from
www.riverbendpublishing.com, 1-866-787-2363.